Flies, Ties,
& Techniques

Flies, Ties,
& Techniques

CHARLES JARDINE

First edition for the United States, its territories and dependencies, and Canada published in 2008 by Barron's Educational Series, Inc.

This book was conceived, designed, and produced by
Ivy Press
The Old Candlemakers,
West Street,
Lewes,
East Sussex, BN7 2NZ, U.K.

All inquiries should be addressed to:
Barron's Educational Series, Inc.
250 Wireless Boulevard
Hauppauge, NY 11788
www.barronseduc.com

ISBN-13: 978-0-7641-3906-2
ISBN-10: 0-7641-3906-1

Library of Congress Control Number: 2007927697

Creative Director: Peter Bridgewater
Publisher: Jason Hook
Editorial Director: Caroline Earle
Senior Project Editor: Dominique Page
Art Director: Sarah Howerd
Designer: Simon Goggin
Project Designer: Kate Haynes
Photographer: Andrew Perris

Printed in China
9 8 7 6 5 4 3 2 1

CONTENTS

INTRODUCTION

Fifty patterns! Just fifty to cover the thousands of designs that have been thrown onto trout and grayling waters worldwide since Aelian's first recorded efforts almost two thousand years ago?

Yes, just the fifty. The strange thing is, when one actually has to work to a very specific brief and concentrate the mind sufficiently to devise a pattern list that ranges across the full spectrum of fly fishing, a sudden truth begins to dawn. Of course favorites will be overlooked and designs peculiar to specific areas—and fishing styles—will be put to one side in favor of generality but, by choosing judiciously, a whole spectrum of methods, materials, and manipulations can be incorporated in a very limited number of designs. This is what I have tried to do here. When it gets right down to it, fly tying is, and always will be, a simple manipulation of materials—winding, spinning, and knotting: that's it, that's all. Of course, these incorporate a host of other factors: there is style—personal, geographical, and regional; there is balance; proportion; coordination; and knowledge about the suitability of certain materials. This, too, is fly tying, but for all the perceived complexity, it remains a very simple business. That is how it started, that is how it remains. Master just the basic principles and then let your imagination—and powers of observation—run riot.

I make no excuse for basing this book firmly in the "bug" camp. The study of insects is not only key in fly fishing, but it's also fundamental to designing and tying flies. Admittedly, in salmon fishing one is looking to attract rather than deceive, and in sea trout and steelhead fishing there is a combination of imitation and attraction involved in fly construction. However, this book is more for the trout and grayling fisher; and I make no excuses for a heavy bias toward fly designs and strategies for fishing them that are firmly rooted in the world of insects and their imitation.

This is a world that is endlessly fascinating and makes sense of what we do, but exactly what route does the fly dresser take? Slavish rendition and close copy accuracy, a calculated middle route conveying the complex in comparative simple terms, or out and out impressionism? The answer is, of course, yes to all three. Fly tying is about breadth and exploration, and about variations on themes. By knowing how to do one style, it is possible to create another. Learn all these styles, as there will be instances that call for this range of possibilities when fishing.

None of us can hope to create and sculpt nature: it is too complex and, yes, perfect. But we can breathe life into the inanimate. That is what we are doing in our little surprise packages, choosing materials that will *react* to the conditions and the water in which we intend the patterns to fish. But this will require some work first. In order to have an idea how to convey the insects in a real or impressionistic manner, it is important to know what that insect or food item actually looks like and how it moves. Too often, fly dressers simply do not know what they are trying to achieve or what the pattern is trying to do. It is like an artist attempting to paint a picture without knowing anything about color. Just watch this living underwater world of food, and you will then see how best to imitate the movement and how to fish the patterns crafted. It is that simple. Honestly.

HOW TO USE THIS BOOK

Wherever I have been able, I have tried to highlight a specific way of tying and, by so doing, to develop a catalog of skills that can be applied over a very wide spectrum of patterns. So, while the idea of just fifty patterns might at first appear ludicrous—and almost an insult to the vast history of fly designs over the centuries—it is actually the signpost and route map to hundreds, possibly thousands, of designs beyond these humble fifty.

Take the Black Magic, a great, simple, and deadly English North Country pattern that captures a huge array of dark-colored creatures trapped in and about the surface of many rivers and lakes in the world. However, with addition of, let us say, a turn of red fluorescent floss or pearl Mylar at the end of the fly's body, you can lift it from one area into another. Adding a microbead might be another way to go, too, offering you a fly pattern that fishes slightly deeper. The whole thing is, ostensibly, the same pattern.

The knowledge of how to turn a hackle for a dry fly can be used to palmer a Woolly Bugger; it is all just hackling. The same goes for dubbing: the choice of dubbing might be specific to certain designs and sizes of fly—soft for small, robust for large—but the actual ways of attaching that dubbing and fashioning a body are basically the same for all flies.

The other element that I am keen for you to grasp—grapple, even—from the book is that fly patterns are like building blocks, and on a simple, but solid, foundation a skyscraper can be constructed. That is why there is, hopefully, some semblance of logical order to the patterns presented here. One simply cannot get away from the fact that if you can wind or cut in a controlled and coordinated manner, you are well on the way to mastering fly tying. I have always suggested that students, certainly at the beginning of the journey, follow simple routes and simple patterns. The temptation, and I know this to my cost (both figuratively and literally), is to start to explore all your avenues from the word "go." This is how the Bloggins Rodent Basher or Curly's Curlew Cluster or some other eponymous nightmare of feathery explosions around the hook comes into being. Learn your craft on the known, the reliables. The growth of your skill base will accelerate and your success with the flies that you tie will be a real revelation, rather than a short-lived thing of not very much at all. This simple building-block route will also assist your understanding of materials and where they can be taken. Once this is known, the learning curve is dramatically steep and the patterns from the jaws of the vise will have resonance, purpose, function, use, and validity—not bad for a simple "belt-and-braces" philosophy.

Two of the key areas for fly tiers everywhere are balance and proportion. Whether you are a newcomer or an old hand, these areas are crucial to the overall "fishability" of a fly and your tying enjoyment, let alone the fly's eventual outcome. The approach and thread management, the point at which the various materials—bulky or not—are then tied and fashioned around a hook, and then the manipulation of those same materials will all be instrumental to the final outcome. Remember, what you put on underneath will affect what goes on thereafter, so an uneven underbody or erratic turns of thread or lead wire will ultimately lead to an uneven body. Why bother? Do the fish care? Well, probably not. That doesn't mean you shouldn't strive to create and craft the best and neatest patterns that you can. Let the trout make them ragged. I have always felt that a fly you are proud of will ultimately lead to a greater degree of success—you will simply fish it with more confidence.

The paths and lessons that you learn, are simple and can lead to some complicated outcomes (we are now back to those foundations again). If you set down deep, robust roots anchored in common sense and proper procedures, you can then explore all other possibilities.

Within these pages a fly pattern's difficulty level is noted down. Accept it and aim for small successes, rather than achieving wholesale failures. I promise that you will get to the tricky stuff much faster and with more confidence.

I will leave you with one cautionary note. You can craft the finest tied flies that have ever tumbled from the grips of a vise jaw, but if you don't know how to fish them or are unable to see those flies through a fish's eyes, then they count for nothing.

CHARLES JARDINE
Banks of the River Severn, England

BASIC SKILLS

TOOLS FOR THE JOB

It is often said that, "It's a poor workman who blames his tools." In fly-tying terms, these tools are often essential and they make the tasks and outcomes so much easier. The axioms "You get what you pay for" and "Get the best you can afford" are entirely appropriate. A few tools will suffice initially, but as you learn and become adept, your tool box will grow exponentially.

YOU WILL NEED

1 A vise
2 A bobbin threader
3 A pair of hackle pliers
4 A range of bobbin holders
5 A good pair of sharp, pointed fly-tier's scissors
6 A popsicle stick coated with Velcro (I kid you not—the best dubbing brush going!)
7 A strong, long, sharply pointed dubbing needle or bodkin
8 A CDC twiddling stick
9 A hair stacker
10 Some fly-tying wax (cobbler's wax)
11 Varnish
12 A small animal fur comb (seriously)
13 A pair of rotational hackle pliers
14 A dubbing loop spinner

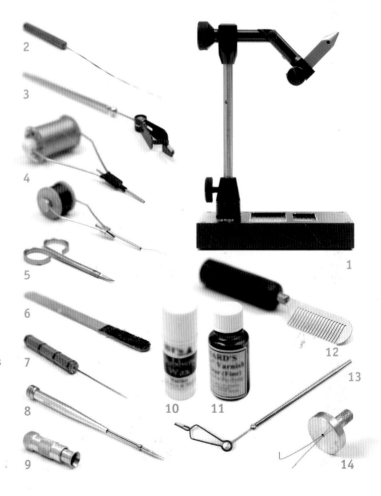

THE BASIC FLY

Waist: Pronounced on this pattern and one of a few that has this.

Wing: Keep in proportion to the rest of the fly—usually, the wing height should not extend further than the length of the hook shank.

Body: The "guts" of the fly, and can be both a suggestion of realism or pure attraction, as is the case here.

Tail: In most cases, the tail should be approximately the length of the hook shank.

Hook eye: Try not to cover this with varnish—it can be very frustrating when at the water's edge!

Hooks: These are vital, of course. This is a typical barbless style. Chose your hook for the task intended and make sure that the weight of "wire" is appropriate for the task.

Hackle: This is a dry fly hackle—and bushy. The length should not usually exceed the gape of the hook by much. Just past is fine.

GETTING STARTED

1 Clamp the hook in the jaws of the vise.

2 Some exponents of the art insist that you should mask the point for fear of the thread being snagged on the sharp metal. I, and others, maintain that doing this makes the job more difficult, and that in any case you will quickly learn to avoid catching the thread on the point of the hook.

3 Fold the thread over the shank of the hook at the eye end. Make sure that enough of the shank remains exposed to leave room to finish the pattern.

4 Still holding the shorter tag end, make very close, tensioned turns with the bobbin holder to trap this tag end, and establish a firm layer of thread along the shank.

5 By holding the tag end of the thread at a steep angle as shown, the wraps of thread being taken down the hook shank by the bobbin can slide down the slope and abut easily, creating a series of tight-touching turns.

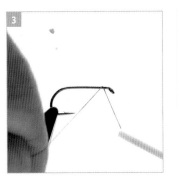

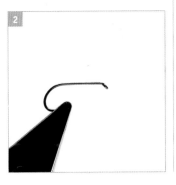

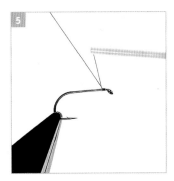

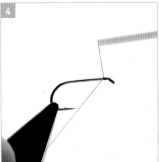

TAILS

These are the support act. They can be long, short, stubby, thin, full, mobile—anything. The important thing is that you keep a sense of proportion in relation to the hook size and the overall appearance of the dressing.

STIFF TAILS

1 Select the minimum amount of material that you think will do the job. Less is more in this game. Offer them up—our funky way of saying, "Take them up to the hook shank and try them out for size!" Ensure that (in the case of dry flies and classic wet flies) the length is about the same as the hook shank. It can be a tiny bit over or under, but this will give you a well-proportioned design; thereafter, it's all a question of "style."

2 Tie these in so that the butt of the tails (the stubby end bit!) is close to the eye. Trim if necessary, but do make sure you cover the tails with a smooth layer of thread. Your mantra in all instances is "No lumps and bumps."

3 In this instance, we are doing a simple divided tail, so prior to the tail being tied in you place a little bit of dubbing (*see page 14*) right on the hook bend.

4 Divide the tailing fibers into two equal portions and continue the thread wraps.

5 Close the thread tightly down along the shank and ensure that it beds into the dubbing ball, causing the fibers to flare.

6 Your divided tail is now complete and should look like this.

Note: If you don't want a divided tail, just omit the dubbing stage and continue the thread wraps to just short of the hook bend. Always remember to leave yourself room to tie in other materials!

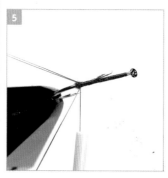

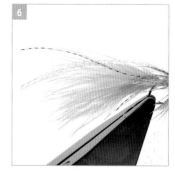

BODIES & RIBS

A lot of work can be achieved by a well-constructed body (wound, dubbed, feather, tinsel, fur—anything in fact that conveys the concept you wish to achieve) followed by a neat and even ribbing process.

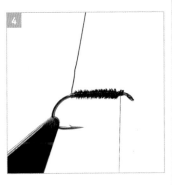

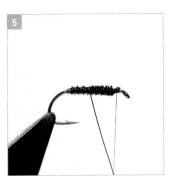

A SIMPLE FEATHER, FLOSS, OR FIBER-WOUND BODY

1 Start the thread as normal and (having tied in a tail, if required) catch in your rib halfway down the shank, be it wire, Mylar, or any other material.

2 Tie in the body material; in this case, feather fiber (pheasant tail).

3 Wind the body. If you want a sparse body, keep the fibers (usually three or four) open and flat. If you want a rounded, almost segmented, body, twist the fibers carefully into a ropelike configuration.

4 Wind the rib in even segment turns up the body. Some tiers prefer to go the same way as the body, which is my preference, as it is far easier to "tie off" and secure.

5 Others wind in the opposite direction to enhance security.

6 It is important to have a mental image of where you want to finish and what comes next: leave room! Secure and tie off.

DUBBING

This needn't strike terror into your heart. All that is required is some well-waxed thread and the right choice of material to dub with. If you are experiencing problems, merely select a material that's more conducive to spinning, such as rabbit

A DUBBED BODY

1 First, make sure your thread is well-waxed.

2 Catch in the rib as normal and take the thread to the point where you want to start the dubbing (the hook bend in this instance). Open up the strands of your chosen dubbing mixture and give them "air." This will allow them to intertwine and lock together more easily. Having waxed your thread, merely place a cluster of fibers along the waxed thread and roll these around the thread between your thumb and forefinger, and in one direction only. This is what I refer to as mono-directional dubbing. The one point that should guide you throughout is "less is more." Like salt in cooking, dubbing can always be added but it's hell to take out!

3 Ensure the strand is evenly wound, taut, and nicely tapered.

4 Wind the rib as shown in neat, even turns.

5 Once you have reached the end of the dubbing and ensured the rib sequence is even, tie off and re-wax the thread in preparation for step 6.

6 If you want to add a thorax, then go through the same procedure as in step 5. Then select some suitable dubbing (in this case, hare's mask fur) that is well mixed. The image clearly shows "the air" I give the dubbing blends. This truly assists it to grip and meld together. Dub in the same way as previously shown.

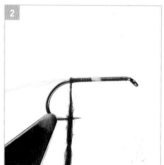

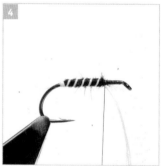

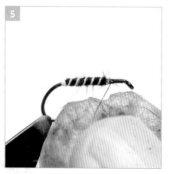

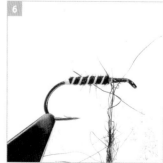

or muskrat. Choose long, rather than short, staple fiber lengths and avoid very hard, unyielding materials, such as Antrons and seal's fur (sub).

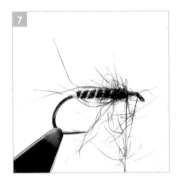

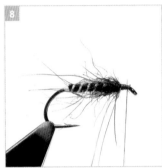

7 Cover the area you have identified, leaving room to finish or add a hackle (*see page 18*).

8 Tease it out to emulate straggly legs or hatching wing case chaos—whatever works. Make it messy though! As a prelude to hackles you might want to continue with this experiment and both dub and create a fur/hair hackle at the same time; so, once the thorax has been dubbed, throw and secure a loop of thread as shown.

9 Grip some long fur fibers (rabbit is great) by their tips in a binder clip.

10 Insert the fibers into the loop using the clip. The loop should be held under tension by a dubbing spinner.

11 Spin the base of the loop and create a whirl of fur through the resultant spirals, which in turn will trap the fibers firmly. This does take some practice, and the odd mistake can lead to domestic tensions, but it is relatively easily learned—honestly.

12 The finished result.

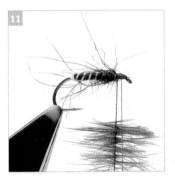

WINGS

Wings are the final flourish on a fly: its crowning glory. They provide mobility and silhouette when wet, and when dry the promise—to the fish—of insectlike food and a target for its attention.

MARABOU/MIXED SOFT FIBERS

1 Select a bunch of marabou (or similar fibers) and offer them up (meaning, take them up to the hook shank and try them out for size). Most fly wings will measure the length of the shank or a little beyond. Now moisten the fingers and rotate the bunch of fibers in a rolling motion between the fingers. This knits the base together, makes it stable, and also reduces the bulk.

2 In the case of marabou, never trim the tips to make them even, but "pinch out" with your finger and thumb. This will maintain the taper of the material.

3 Make some wraps to secure the gathered fibers at the base.

4 Trim the ends.

5 Make successive wraps and ensure that the entire area is smooth.

6 Now, as a flourish, you can add another element—maybe some jungle cock eyes on either side to create one of the more deadly stillwater flies of recent times, the Cormorant.

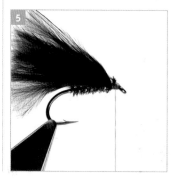

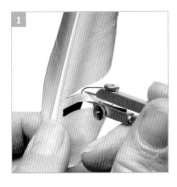

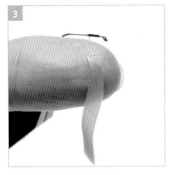

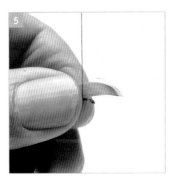

QUILL DRY FLY WING

Select a wing that will tie in easily. Mallard is one of the easier ones. Make sure you pair the quills and use thread that is well-waxed. So…let the adventure begin.

1 With a pair of dividers or anything that will provide a way of creating equal segments, separate the quill sections. Choose an area that will curve outward and be easy to hold together. Avoid straight segments and long lower quill areas.

2 This area on the secondary mallard quills is ideal—a "sweet spot" of sorts.

3 When picking up the quill segments to match them tip to tip, it is best to moisten your finger tips and dab these on the quill. They will come up easily. Now just place them tip to tip so they match.

4 Offer the paired segments up to the hook and make sure they are as long as the shank. This is the guideline: the wing height should be the length of the hook shank.

5 Following a similar procedure to the wet fly (see page 18), but with the dry fly wing paired and facing to the front of the hook and over the eye, pull the thread between your finger and thumb—the well-waxed thread, that is!

6 Make sure that the thread is between that finger and thumb and that the quill wing is supported on top of the hook. I find that it helps to have the wing slightly biased toward my side of the hook, as the thread turn pressure will then tend to centralize it.

7 Make a rotation of the thread around the wing to the far side, then pull the thread smoothly upward. This is a fairly unusual way of doing this maneuver, but one that seems to bring the thread downward on the quill more firmly and in a better position. Try it.

8 Hoist the wing upward and make turns in front of the wing to secure it in the upright position—not behind, as this will disrupt the segments and cause the wing to twist.

WET FLY WING

1 Start with a feather that is conducive to this style. Game bird wings are great and so are some domestic fowl. Whichever feather you select, make sure that the fibers "zip" and "lock" together. Make sure, too, that you have a paired wing of equal length and depth. In this instance, I have selected a hen pheasant wing.

2 Bring the pairs together tip to tip and, using well-waxed thread, offer them up and "pinch and loop" or "soft loop" them in.

3 Be bold: with it between your finger and thumb, pull the thread firmly downward with the bobbin.

4 If you have been bold and the thread has been waxed sufficiently, the result should look like this.

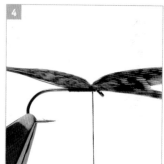

HACKLING

Creating a hackle can be confusing to the newcomer, yet is invariably easier than first supposed. There are disarmingly few styles: there is parachute hackling, which we will cover later in the book (see page 64). Then there is the classic wound style, which can apply to both soft hackles and "hard" hackles.

1 Look for the start of the sweet spot, the point at which the webby fibers next to the stem give way to clean, stiff fibers that extend almost from stem to point.

2 Raise up the webby fibers and trim off if necessary.

3 Now measure the fiber for balance by bending the stem and allowing the fibers to flare outward. They should be about the same length as the hook gape, the distance between the hook shank and the hook point.

4 The finished fly. A well-hackled fly will lift anything around it and make it appear special.

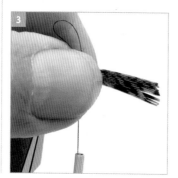

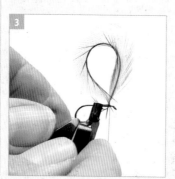

RIVER RELIABLES
BELOW THE SURFACE

DAN BYFORD

Season: All
Type of fish: Most predatory

ZONKER

This pattern is one of truly international status and, while it's used widely throughout the rough-and-tumble rivers of the Western U.S. particularly, it has origins firmly entrenched in the New Zealand Rabbit Series of patterns popularized in the U.K. by John Veniard's books of the '70s. Now it is seen as a first-choice pattern for almost any "bait-fish" situation.

DIFFICULTY 7/10

MAKING THE FLY

1 Layer the thread on the hook, tie in the tailing materials, and then add the turns of lead wire to the middle of the hook shank.

2 Tie in the body material and then make a smooth taper on either side of the lead wire turns. This will ensure that the Mylar runs the length of the hook shank without the "gremlins" of "lumps and bumps." Take the Mylar up and down the shank about three times to craft a ridge-free body.

3 Dub the thorax—make sure that you leave room to add the wing.

4 Prepare the Zonker strip by "pointing" the end that will project over the hook bend—this seems to add a dimension of movement to the design when actually fishing.

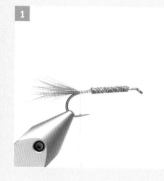

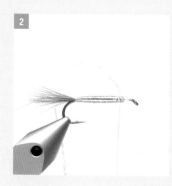

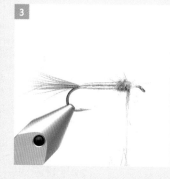

The secret of the pattern's success probably lies in a combination of factors: bulk and the contour of a small prey species, plus the lustrous sinewy movement of the rabbit fur that can prove the undoing of some of the largest fish in the stream. Big fly = big fish! Recently it has enjoyed considerable success on stillwaters, too, spawning any number of slimmer variations substituting mink for the ubiquitous rabbit wing—often this variation is seen as the ultimate fly pattern and especially when the quarry wants its patterns fished very slowly. I would honestly regard this pattern (in its variations) as one of the "must have" designs for almost any fly box anywhere in the world.

Hook: Long shank 2–12 weighted with turns of lead wire to match the diameter of the hook wire

Thread: Black or tan 6/0

Tail: Cock hackle fibers (approx. 20) in orange, red, or olive

Rib: Gold or silver wire, fine/medium depending on hook size

Body: Pearl Mylar

Thorax (optional): Red dubbing

Wing: Pre-cut Zonker strip—rabbit or mink/squirrel (for smaller hook sizes)

Collar (optional): Rabbit fur from strip

Head: Roman Moser "snap" head or merely a build up of fly-tying thread formed into a smooth shape

MATERIALS

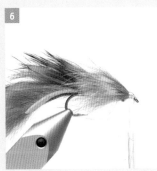

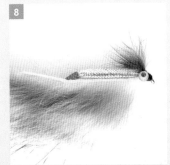

5 Secure the thicker end at the hook eye and then fold the strip along the back of the shank. Make a securing turn around the strip with the wire rib at the hook bend. Moisten your fingers and ease the fur fibers back against the nap to expose the skin and continue the wire turns in an even manner in the style known as "Matuka."

6 This part is optional. Trim a bunch of fur from the skin and tie this in a circle around the head area as a "collar."

7 Add a Roman Moser "snap" head "eye" and secure in place with instant glue, or build up a head of thread and anoint with a high-gloss varnish.

8 Another way of crafting the Zonker. By securing the strip through the hook point and bringing the fur along the underside of the hook the fly will fish hook point uppermost.

A big brown trout lurking near the bottom of a river—a perfect target for the Zonker.

TACTICS

This pattern can be fished on a sunk line, floating line in fast water, slow water, stillwater: you name it. However, its true strength lies in its ability to attract very large trout—often those that aggressively chase down "bait" fish. One favorite method is to fish the Zonker across relatively shallow water—if possible wading out from the bank, then casting into the bank as close as you can, paying attention to rocks, fallen logs, overhanging bushes, or scrub willow (anything that could be a hideout for a reluctant trout). When fishing this pattern on rivers make sure there is sufficient weight to get the fly to where it matters—the bottom layer. Then grip and ride the current, animating the design with short jerks via the line hand or slow pulls so that it darts and flits like a living creature.

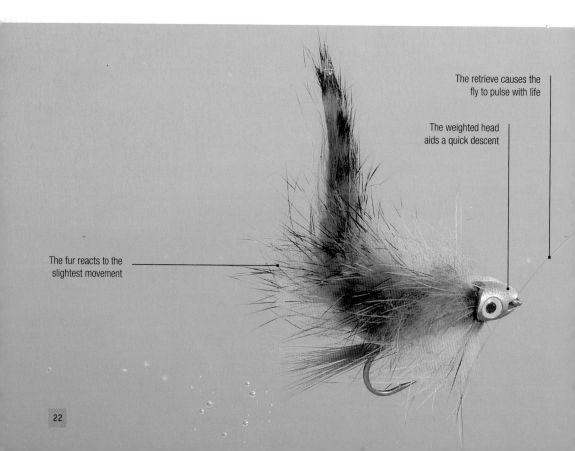

The retrieve causes the fly to pulse with life

The weighted head aids a quick descent

The fur reacts to the slightest movement

BEHAVIOR

The way to understand how to tie and fish this pattern is to look at small fish, either in a river or an aquarium. Look at their movement: the way in which they grip the current, dart under rocks, sway with the force of water. Then, all you have to do is to build this into your angling repertoire. So few people bother to understand how their fly will fish. They spend inordinate amounts of time (and money) in collecting materials, hours at the vise, perfecting technique, agonizing over what system to fish the fly on, practice casting, then when they're near water and ready to fish the darn thing, they just throw it out and switch off. My advice is to live in the moment; mentally try to climb below or on top (if you are fishing a floating design) of the surface and imagine what your fly is doing at any given moment: sense it. That way you will bring variety of movement to the retrieve, you will sense the "fold" of water around line and fly. You will be at one with the whole thing. And you will definitely sense the fish and the take!

A Zonker is equally effective for fry-feeding fish on stillwater. Proof, too, that "matching the hatch" is not just confined to flies!

TACKLE
This is not a fly for the dry fly outfit! Big flies need heavy gear, not because the fish will be any bigger—though indeed they might be—but purely because you have a heavy payload to wield about in the air. If I were using a size 6 Zonker I would definitely look to a #6 9 ft (2.7 m) rod. If I thought the volume of water demanded additional weight, I might even consider a #7. Most lines are floating but do carry the occasional sunk line or wet-tip in really fast currents. Leaders I keep fairly short because of the likelihood of "hinging"—the heavy fly hinging with the fly line during the cast. I would also consider using split shot/sinkers on the leader if I needed to get lower in the water column. Tippet sizes should be a minimum of 4X, and I see good reason to use 2X.

VARIATIONS
Experiment with various animal fur strips in the wing. Rabbit is the staple but try mink, squirrel, fitch—anything that has a well-tanned soft hide and looks mobile.

WOOLLY BUGGER

RUSSELL BLESSING

Season: All
Type of fish: All game fish species
(including grayling occasionally!)

This pattern, with all its many color variations, is probably the one that more anglers have used to catch their first trout than any other—a bold statement, but one that bears scrutiny, judging by most fly boxes and fishing catalogs. Like the Zonker, it is a journeyman of the waters; its home is, frankly, anywhere it is fished, and its effectiveness in a multiplicity of roles is legendary.

DIFFICULTY 5/10

MAKING THE FLY

1 Thread a bead—copper or gold, either tungsten or brass—on the hook. Attach the thread.

2 Place the weight more to the middle to achieve a better sink path. Coat with a layer of instant glue to support it. Build up the head and tail with thread wraps to form a neat taper. Add additional weight for deep water and fast flows.

3 Now tie in the marabou fibers immediately behind the bead and then, with touching turns, trap the fibers down toward the bend. Add the rib.

4 Strip the fibers off of the chenille to expose the cotton core and tie these in at the hook bend. Then add the cock hackle at the bead-head end.

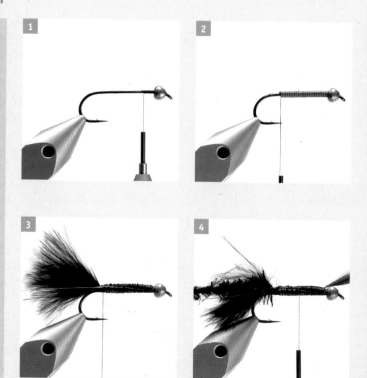

This is a pattern that can look like almost anything. It has a buzz of life about it and fish like it. There's movement, and an outline that converts into many different fish food items. Whether you are fishing in a river or a lake, it is another "must-have, must-use" pattern. Recently, this style has found great success—especially in olive variation—on British lakes, where it can be used as an impressionistic pattern to imitate damsel nymphs and so on. On streams it can suggest small fish, leeches, large mayfly sp. such as *Isonychia* and green and brown drakes (in appropriate colors), hellgrammites, and many others. One not to leave home without.

Hook: Most—long shank and standard 2–12
Weight: Optional—gold bead and lead (sub) wire
Thread: Black/olive/claret/red 6/0
Tail: Marabou
Rib: Gold, copper, or silver oval tinsel
Body: Chenille
Hackle: Palmered cock hackle
Collar: Optional—contrasting dubbing

MATERIALS

5 Wind the chenille in very close touching turns up the hook shank in a way that maintains bulk.

6 Palmer the cock hackle in even, open turns down the hook shank, winding it carefully "through" the chenille wraps.

7 Trap the palmered hackle with even, neat wraps of the ribbing material. Secure immediately behind the bead.

8 Having secured the rib, cover the resultant thread wraps with a flourish of contrasting dubbing—pink with red strands works superbly.

A Bugger-caught brown returned to its home on the White River Arkansas.

TACTICS

Similar to the Zonker, think of a situation and the chances are the Woolly Bugger will meet it. While this section is primarily about river fishing, it should not be forgotten what a truly excellent impressionistic design this is on stillwater, too. And that is the essence of the pattern: easy to tie versatility—an "if in doubt, tie it on" sort of pattern. So how do you fish it? I would opt for the same styles as outlined for the Zonker. However, there are times, especially if you tether a small-length light tippet to the hook bend and a smaller pattern to this, when you can dead drift as one might a large nymph—especially stone flies or hellgrammites and other large dark subsurface river dwellers. Fish the fly behind boulders, in riffles, and other boisterous areas. Of course, there is always the fail-me-not-cast: cast square to you, let the current grip the line and swing, river-flow aided, around in a fish-enticing arcing curve. It is a lot of fun, but don't overlook the dead drift.

The marabou tail reacts to the smallest movement

The bead head helps the fly to sink rapidly

The palmered hackle gives a "buzz" of life

BEHAVIOR

This pattern relies on two key elements: "bulk"—the actual dense silhouette—and "mobility"—the filigree of palmered hackle that pulses in the current and the sinuous, lithe nature of marabou. This means that this is an all-action, all-moving pattern that almost dances through the layers. And it is this movement that emulates a whole host of creatures—from damsel nymphs to small fish to stoneflies, dragonflies, and so on. All of us are taken with the idea of recreating nature—tying flies that actually look like the insects they purport to represent. Yet the reality is different. Build in the triggers of movement and you will have a much better fly design. The Woolly Bugger (in its many guises and coats) has movement in abundance.

This classic West Country (U.K.) brown fell victim to the dark destroyer—the Woolly Bugger.

TACKLE
Because of the weight and the bulk it is advisable to use fly rods in the region of 9 ft (2.7 m) and lines of #6 and up—and don't forget to carry either full sunk lines or weighted leaders.

VARIATIONS
Colors can be variegated. Good ones, apart from the obligatory black, are olive and brown. Try brighter ones—a purple and black version is often used for steelhead.

KAUFMANN STONE

There are hundreds of stonefly nymph designs. It is a fly that brings out the best—and the worst—in fly dressers. The realistic tiers will home in on all the lovely neo-primal parts: legs and body armor such as segmentation, wing cases, and so on. The impressionists, too, will enjoy the shape, but also the "buggyness." And the trout? Well, they just like to eat them.

RANDALL KAUFMANN

Season: Late spring and summer
Type of fish: Primarily trout

DIFFICULTY 7/10

MAKING THE FLY

1 Place the hook in the vise—and here a good vise that really grips the hook is truly essential.

2 Now take a flame to the thoracic area of the hook. Hold it to the wire to soften it, and then carefully bend it as shown with forceps.

3 Allow the hook to cool, attach the thread in the usual way, and then add the biot tails and antennae.

4 Add the vinyl rib, fashion the dubbing in tight mono dub (*see page 14*) around the thread, and start making touching turns up the shank.

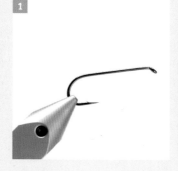

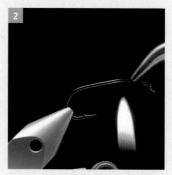

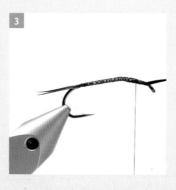

This pattern, as its name suggests, is a lover of swift rivers. It is a specific creature, but it is found in many parts of the trout fisher's world. It is also a great pattern for overcoming the vagaries of current; this design can pack an awful lot of lead and reach the riverbed where the naturals lurk. It is also a good design to fish in conjunction with a smaller nymph—a Brassie or similar. And what about the recent addition of rubber legs? Well, they add movement and "kick" to the design (similarly to the Girdle Bug series and Bitch Creeks), thereby elevating the effectiveness further. Also try smaller amber, brown, and other colored variations to meet a world of stonefly options.

Hook: Long shank 4–12 weighted with turns of lead (sub) wire

Thread: Black claret or amber 6/0

Tail and antennae: Goose biots in appropriate colors, e.g. black

Legs: Rubber legs (Rainy's, etc.), three on each side of the thorax (original did not have these)

Rib: Oval nylon/v-rib clear or opaque black, amber, or brown

Body: Seal's fur (sub) to match the natural. The blend for black is 80% black, 10% orange, 5% purple, 5% dark brown

Thorax band: Orange dubbing

Wing case: Shaped oak turkey wing fibers

MATERIALS

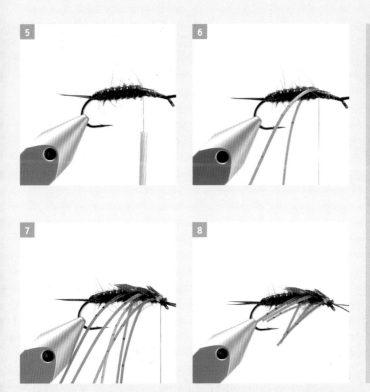

5 Rib the abdomen with neat, open turns. Proportions are vital here: do not go past the two-thirds mark.

6 Add the rubber legs in three sections through the thorax with diagonal crosses of thread wraps.

7 Having previously trimmed the wing-cases to an appropriate shape, create the thorax in three separate sections. The sequence, working up the hook, is to dub between the second and third pairs of legs, tie in the clipped wing case, then repeat two more times.

8 Dub at the head area to finish the whole thing off, and then trim the rubber legs very carefully and evenly.

TACTICS

While this type of pattern and fishing are often identified with the bruising rivers of the Western U.S., wherever you have freestone types of water and a stonefly population, a fly like this will work.

I prefer a floating line, a longish leader, and this pattern with a bead Troth Pheasant Tail (*see page 36*) on a small length of tippet attached to the hook bend, so that the combination swirls around the pockets, eddies, and subsurface structure of the riverbed.

The typical speed, depth, and water type for a variety of stonefly species. A place where a nymph can be fished with confidence almost throughout the season—way beyond the accepted hatch period.

The dubbing grips air bubbles like a real nymph

The rubber legs "kick" with life

The weight slows it to fish near the bottom

BEHAVIOR

The natural nymph has a two-year lifecycle and tends to hatch out from mid-June to mid-July by climbing along the riverbed stones and onto the bankside rocks and other structures. The fly, though, has a far more protracted use than that, and this nymph can be fished in any fast pocket of water or riffle with confidence, especially in the combination suggested. You are trying to emulate a fly that has been dislodged from its sanctuary on and among the subsurface rocks.

A typical example of the Perlidae *sp.—a group of stoneflies that offer the fly fisher some seriously sizable creatures to imitate and fish: some as large as size 2 long shank!*

TACKLE

As in the case of the Woolly Bugger, you would be well advised to use a heavy nymphing outfit, a #6 being far better than a #5. You might even go to a #7. Many anglers, years ago, used fast-sinking shooting heads to ensure that the patterns reached the bottom, but given the current weighting options—beads and so on—and advanced leaders, this can be done just as easily with a floating line. Fishing the pattern slightly up, across, and down is the way to go—you will achieve maximum depth and then movement.

VARIATIONS

None, other than color: dark brown, amber, tan dubbed body, but with several other colors worked in to add "life" (claret, orange, rust, purple, ginger, crimson, and so on).

DOUG PRINCE

Season: All
Type of fish: Primarily trout
and grayling

PRINCE NYMPH

The Prince Nymph is one of those patterns that covers a multitude of sins and retains an air of singular attraction at the same time. It's a peculiar combination. There are others: Gold Ribbed Hare's Ear, Pheasant Tail, Diawl Bach, to name just a few. All pretty much say to the quarry, "OK, here I am; now you make up your mind what it is you think that I look like in food terms." They're good flies to have in the box, I assure you, to take away the agonies of decision-making!

DIFFICULTY 5/10

MAKING THE FLY

1 Place a bead on the hook, run touching turns of thread to seven-eighths of the way down the shank and catch in two biots. Make sure that the flare is outward and the tips are even, and then tie in some oval gold tinsel.

2 Take the thread back to the rear of the bead, add a brown cock hackle, and then twist some lead wire midships (optional).

3 Secure two strands of peacock herl by their tips between the end of the lead wire wraps and the biot tails.

4 Twist and spin the strands of peacock herl around the tying thread (using the thread as a spine) to form a tightly furled rope effect.

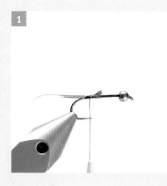

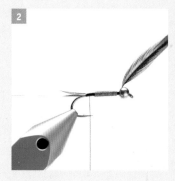

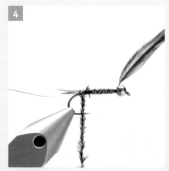

The thing about the Prince Nymph is that it could look like a cased caddis—I believe that it was intended to be either a stonefly design or hellgrammite (Dobson fly) imitation. Then again, trout and grayling might just like the color combination. Who knows? Certainly the combination of red/brown and peacock is a recurring effective theme that flows through the history of the sport. Sometimes it's wise not to ask too many questions of the trout and their preferences...and just go fish!

Hook: Long shank 8–14 (weighted with turns of lead wire)
Bead: Gold (optional)
Thread: Black or brown 8/0
Hackle: Natural red
Tail: Brown goose biot
Rib: Oval gold
Body: Wound peacock herl
Wing: White goose biot
Collar: Peacock Ice Dub

MATERIALS

5 Wrap this "rope" in touching turns to a point just short of the bead.

6 Select a pair of white biots and match them so the tips are even; tie these on top of the hook shank, so that the natural curve of the biot sweeps upwards (concave). The tip of the biot should finish at the bend or close to the tail tips.

7 Wind the hackle and sweep it back in an almost wet-fly style.

8 Mask the thread wraps and build up by the bead by adding a little Ice Dubbing or similar peacock orientated sparkle dubbing.

TACTICS

This is primarily an impressionistic pattern designed to fish in and around the bottom area of fast-flowing rivers. As I have already mentioned, it is quite deadly when used in conjunction with a dry fly, but it also works well in just a plain upstream nymphing role.

On stillwaters, use this pattern as a point fly, with a smaller midge pupa perhaps, just above on a dropper. When fishing from the bank or in a fairly stationary boat or float tube, allow it to be curved around on the wind with a floating line and a long leader.

Classic riffly water, where the Prince Nymph is the perfect "search" pattern.

The air bubble looks like a real insect's internal gases

The bead helps sink the fly and gives an illusion of life

BEHAVIOR

Because of the fly's inherent weight, it fishes near the bottom. And that is its role—to emulate creatures near the lake or riverbed. The hackle, though, does give it pulse and movement, as do the filigreelike fibers on the sides of the peacock herl. The white flash of the biot on top is widely thought to represent the *Isonychia* nymph's light abdominal linear flash. It could be, though, that trout—and other species—can see the pattern clearly in the murky lower water column. Oddly, on stillwater especially, the design could equally represent many dragonfly nymph species. A pattern to pin faith on.

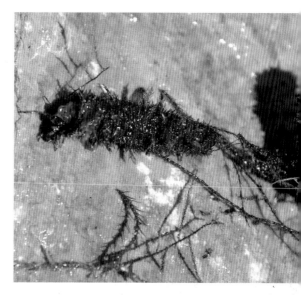

A cased caddis: one of the many creatures imitated by the Prince Nymph.

TACKLE

Because of the wide roles that the pattern covers, you have to be equally broad with the tackle you use. However, I have found a 9 ft 6 in (2.85 m) #6 rod and line on stillwaters—possibly a 10 ft (3 m) #5 on rivers—to be very useful and to offer the degree of water control that many of the techniques require.

VARIATIONS

Many years ago I came up with a pattern called the "Hairy Prince" for fishing on stillwaters; it worked well—and continues to do so. In fact, it has found a niche on rivers, where it suggests a wide number of cased caddis species. The design has a fluorescent green tag and a dubbed hare's ear body. Doug Prince also tied variations—one incorporating a similar design with a black ostrich herl body and a black tail (I think this was the original to the concept). This, too, has worked well for me.

AL TROTH

Season: All
Type of fish: Trout, grayling,
and most other fish!

TROTH PHEASANT TAIL

The world's favorite nymph? Probably. Sentimentally, I should opt for the Frank Sawyer dressing as the lead pattern. I grew up with Frank's pattern, Frank gave me my first "official" casting lessons, and I idolized the man. He was a genius and he understood the aquatic world of spring creeks probably better than any person there has ever been. So why choose another version?

DIFFICULTY 4/10

MAKING THE FLY

1 With the hook in the vise, tie in a group of even cock pheasant tail fiber tips—four or five should do it. Make sure that you use (if you can get them) fibers from mature older birds, because these have better structure and depth of color.

2 Taking the fibers down the shank with touching turns of thread, tie in a length of copper wire or gold tinsel for the rib as you go.

3 Now tie in, by the very end of the tips, four to six more cock pheasant tail fiber strands of the same quality. I tend to trim the very tips so that I get an even tie-in and neatness right at the hook bend.

4 Open up the pheasant tail fibers so that when you wind them forward they will form a smooth, even layer. I try not to twist the strands together, because this adds bulk.

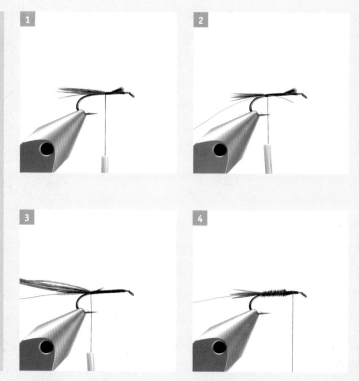

Primarily because it is more versatile. I also think that it meets with the approval of trout and related species over a slightly wider spectrum and can cope with the demands of more water types. It is great on smooth, spring-creek types of water, good on faster, freestone waters, and can be deadly on stillwaters. I also believe that it conveys more species of insects in a loose way. I have found this pattern, especially a version with a pearl flashback in small sizes (16–20), to be deadly in conjunction with a Kaufmann Stone, or similar weighted pattern. Better still, carry both designs!

Hook: 10–18 (weighted with copper wire or lead, or a bead if you must)

Thread: Claret or black 8/0

Tail: Cock pheasant tail fibers: 4 or 5

Rib: Copper wire or fine oval gold tinsel

Body: Cock pheasant tail fibers (4–6 strands)

Thorax cover: Cock pheasant tail fibers (8–10)

Thorax: Peacock herl (try tying in two small rubber legs before winding the thorax for great results!)

Sawyer version: Using just copper wire and cock pheasant tail fibers makes this pattern simpler, leaner, and better suited to clear, smooth water.

MATERIALS

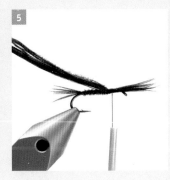

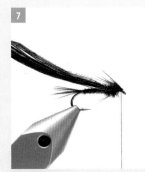

5 Take another bunch of pheasant tail fibers—this time about eight to ten—and tie them in so that the even tips project over the hook eye; these will be bent back to form the hackle, so they should not reach further than halfway down the shank.

6 Wind a thorax of two strands of peacock herl and tie in at the head.

7 Fold the pheasant tail fibers back in two equal clusters, either side of the thorax, and secure in place with thread wraps.

8 Advance the pheasant tail fiber butts forward to make a thorax case, and secure and finish the fly with firm and disciplined even turns of thread. (Pheasant tail can be remarkably unruly to secure at this point, so be careful.)

Home of the Pheasant Tail—an upper Avon grayling comes to the net at Wishford in Wiltshire, U.K.

TACTICS

It would be easy to say that you can fish a Pheasant Tail in any way you want, either on a river or a lake, but that would be missing the point of the design. The essence of fishing this pattern lies in its origins on the streams of Wiltshire and the upper Avon in the U.K. Here, Frank Sawyer developed a way of fishing that has come to be known as the "upstream nymph" or "Netheravon style": assessing a trout's depth and casting sufficiently far ahead to allow the pattern to sink to the trout's depth, then, at the last moment, agitating the fly away from the quarry with a deft flick of the rod tip in a move that has come to be called the "induced take." Fish hate the idea of food getting away from them when they are about to eat it! While this is the Troth version of Frank's fly, I feel sure he would forgive me this once.

The slim profile suggests food and little threat to the quarry

The fly in the dead-drift position

BEHAVIOR

Because of its versatility, there is no one set pattern of behavior with this fly. However, you should try, wherever possible, to emulate the creatures it purports to represent—namely, Olive nymphs. But given its various roles, frankly, if you decide to rip it back at Mach 2 (and I have done this!) it can work. Strange—but effective! While, the P.T. Nymph, as it is affectionately known, covers a multitude of entomological "sins," its true role is imitating many of the upwing (mayfly) species in the nymph form, and then the slimmer ones like the depicted *Baetid* sp. The great thing about a design like this is that it conveys so much with so little, and the trout (and grayling) are seldom alarmed by a P.T. coming into the eye-line—quite the reverse in fact, they positively relish the culinary possibilities!

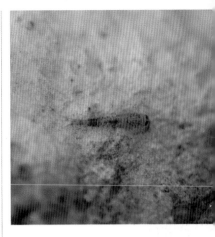

For once, this little mayfly nymph is actually at rest, and "in denial" of its title—Agile Darter! This group of mayfly nymphs account for a large percentage of food for spring creek trout and grayling and are therefore important to imitate.

TACKLE

While it does suit lighter lines—below, say, #6—I know many fishers who use this pattern on heavier outfits in conjunction with streamers and all sorts. Honestly, it is a pattern that you can just go out and fish. Use it with confidence in almost any water type and condition, perhaps with the exception of a massive flood!

VARIATIONS

• Try putting a bead at the head.
• Some people tie in three pheasant tail fibers on each side behind the eye, as a final step, to form the nymph's legs.
• Try a pearl thorax case, instead of pheasant tail.
• Try almost anything with this context—it will probably work!

HARE'S EAR NYMPH

ATTRIBUTED TO JAMES OGDEN, 1879, BUT OLDER HARE'S EAR PATTERNS EXIST

Season: All

Type of fish: Almost any fish you can think of!

I may have been wrong about the Pheasant Tail; the Hare's Ear is also a definite contender for most-used-and-loved nymph. It's a close call. On balance, though, given its buggy outline, the Hare's Ear probably conveys more general food forms than the Pheasant Tail—indeed, this combination of materials surpasses almost any other for sheer impressionistic attraction to the fish.

DIFFICULTY 4/10

MAKING THE FLY

1 Attach the thread to the hook followed by turns of lead wire within the middle part of the hook area. This will ensure evenness when sinking.

2 In the gap to the bend of the hook attach the tail. Be careful to align the tips of the hare's mask fur to form the tail—they can be unruly. Take your time. This is an imprecise art!

3 Add the oval gold tinsel and work the thread in the area between the lead wire and the bend to craft a smooth taper. Note: You should do this at both ends. Be guided by the axiom, "Tie a neat fly and let the fish make it ragged!"

4 Wax the thread, loosely dub a mixture of hare's mask and ear fur on the thread, and then take this up the body in touching turns for two-thirds of its length.

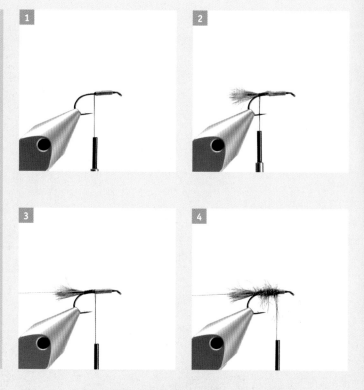

The brindled tans, fawns, browns, and dark accents can suggest a scud (shrimp), sow bug (hog louse), sedge larva or pupa, and many rotund lighter mayfly species—indeed, any that are at the point of emergence. In some cases it can even convey a small fish or other creature. There have been many times when I have been in doubt what to put on the end of my tippet—a Hare's Ear is never far from my thoughts. Heck, I have even caught bonefish on a Hare's Ear! Why? Because it's buggy. This is the classic version; there are many other possibilities and designs, including the ultra-thin versions tied by British stillwater guru Rob Barden.

Hook: Standard or long shank 6–18, weighted as desired
Bead: Optional
Thread: Black, claret, or tan 8/0
Hackle: Optional—red game cock soft hackle
Tail: Aligned fibers from hare's cheek (ensure that there are black tips)
Rib: Oval gold tinsel for larger sizes; wire for smaller
Body: Well mixed hare's ear and mask fur
Wing case: Cock pheasant tail fibers
Thorax: Same as for body

MATERIALS

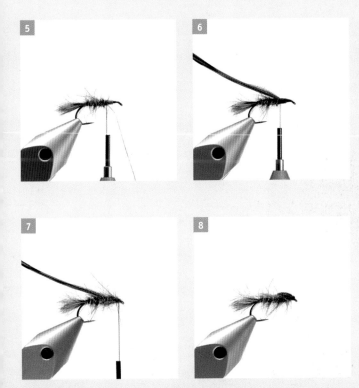

5 Rib the body in the same direction as the turns of dubbing.

6 Now add the pheasant tail thorax cover. Use about eight strands and make sure that these are tied flat and on top of the thorax, otherwise you will get bulk and it will twist and migrate to the far side of the hook.

7 Dub the thoracic area with the same blend and in the same way.

8 Fold over the pheasant tail thoracic cover and tie down, ensuring the fibers are eased slightly toward you to allow for the thread pressure taking them to the far side. Be careful, too, with the thread wraps. Pheasant tail is quite slippery, and if you are not careful with your turns you will end up with the fibers springing free of the thread wraps, ruining the fly.

TACTICS

The texture and color of the natural material lend themselves to two distinct fishing methods. First, near the surface where they can mimic the aspects of the fly (sedge, mayfly, or midge) in the process of hatching, the exoskeleton being discarded and the mess and residual nymphal skin left behind. This approach demands a lightweight version fished virtually static on a long leader and floating line in the surface—a perfect lake-based strategy. The second approach is to fish lower down the water column with a heavier-weighted, slightly more rotund design, especially upstream and dead drift, on rivers (spring creeks) where it is invariably taken for a sow or cress bug, scud, or other bottom-dwelling trout food. Again, long leaders and floating lines are the way to go here.

A Pennsylvanian spring creek rainbow comes to hand—the Gold Ribbed Hare's Ear is a perfect choice to mimic the colonies of scuds found in these waters.

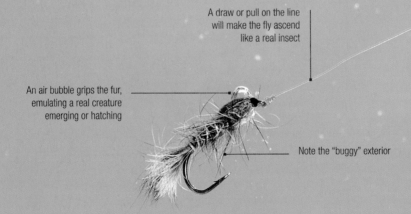

A draw or pull on the line will make the fly ascend like a real insect

An air bubble grips the fur, emulating a real creature emerging or hatching

Note the "buggy" exterior

BEHAVIOR

There is a great deal of merit in having something disheveled in your fly box. Something, in fact, that looks as though there has been an explosion around the hook shank. The Hare's Ear in its many guises allows you to explore a whole mass of different "bug" oriented options, from immediately below the surface to right down to the base layers. Because of the disheveled appearance and the fact that it is so "buggy," rather than plummeting through the layers it will sort of tumble (if weighted) or almost hover (if unweighted). For this reason it not only behaves in a very natural way, but can also tempt fish by doing nothing at all. This is a persuasive argument for carrying both weighted and unweighted designs.

A lovely Italian Fario del Cavaione—or brown trout—taken from the head waters of Valsesia in the country's northern Alpine region. It is trout that has fashioned a tradition of fly fishing for over 400 years on these beautiful snowfield-fueled waters.

TACKLE

As in the case of the Pheasant Tail, you are totally unrestricted on the style of approach or tackle. Just match the size of the fly to the appropriate outfit.

VARIATIONS

The variations on this pattern are worth a book, but I urge you to try the Barden style—this imitates small cress bugs, sow bugs, and even *chironomids* very well. Also, a dry version with a natural red hackle is just great for fast water, giving an impression of a hatching caddis or mayfly.

BRET SMITH

Season: All

Type of fish: Trout, grayling, and many other small fly-loving species (pan fish, etc.)

BRASSIE

This is truly one of those "must-have" designs that meets so many instances that you encounter on the riverbank or on stillwaters. The pattern's original intention was to imitate caddis, but I have found it far better for fish that are feeding on the larvae of a wide range of midges (*chironomid* species) because the shape is representative of many aquatic species in the larval stage. It is a pattern that therefore tends to be taken confidently.

DIFFICULTY 3/10

MAKING THE FLY

1 Attach the thread and make several anchoring wraps in the thoracic area. Now tie in the colored wire on the facing side.

2 With very close, touching turns of thread, trace the contour of the hook, securing the wire as you go. Do not allow the wire to twist and "migrate" to the top or far side.

3 Having taken the wire around the hook bend, make a firm and positional turn with the wire.

4 Continue the wire turns to the thoracic area. Now take several securing turns of thread and lock the wire in place. Remove the wire by agitating it back and forth to rupture. This way you will not ruin your scissors or leave a sharp end on the wire to sever your thread.

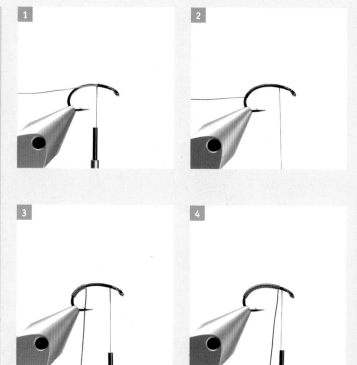

In smaller sizes, this design has fooled some very selective feeders; its simplicity represents a mass of insect complexity. On stillwaters, especially in larger sizes, it has become a hugely successful pattern in the early part of the season for the larger, darker midge—the inherent weight in the body material positioning the fly in the target zone of lower depths. The Brassie is another very useful design to fish in conjunction with a larger, weightier design, to take it through the depths and present a small pattern closer to the riverbed in fast flows.

Hook: Curved grub/scud 10–22

Bead: Copper/gold (optional)

Thread: Black/claret 8/0

Body: Copper wire (to match hook diameter) in colored or copper

Thorax: Black dubbing followed by peacock herl

MATERIALS

5 Tie in two strands of peacock herl and then attach some black soft animal dubbing.

6 Neatly dub the thoracic area with a mono-directional standard dub—or noodle dub for a tighter, neater finish.

7 Form a rope with strands of peacock herl by rotating them around the thread in a tight twist.

8 Wind the peacock herl "rope" immediately after the dubbed thorax and whip finish and varnish. (If you are using a bead, you do all this to the rear of the bead, of course.)

TACTICS

This fly has the capacity for meeting the demands of some often difficult situations in both still and running water. I think the primary reason is that it can resemble many types of food forms and not shriek a warning of "impostor" to the fish. I have found on British stillwaters that, when used to target individual fish—spotting a cruising trout, assessing its depth, then casting sufficiently far ahead for the trout to sidle up and meet the tiny fly that has intercepted its cruise pattern—the Brassie is seldom refused. Because it can convey so much with so little that it looks innocuous, it can be hung from behind a larger nymph—a Kaufmann Stone, Zonker, Woolly Bugger, almost anything—on a small length of tippet attached to the larger fly's hook bend. Then tempt the trout attracted to (and maybe slightly wary of) the bigger pattern, and let it be beguiled by the smaller fly.

The author's son, Alex, surveys a U.K. chalk stream—ideal for fishing a small Brassie.

The wire body helps the fly to cut through the surface

The slim curved shape represents many subsurface insects

BEHAVIOR

Life below surface, we must assume, is often seen by fish in a fleeting way. A sudden darting form that is either fairly robust and portly, or slim and lithe; good to eat, not good to eat. It is doubtful that trout can deduce legs, eyes, antennae, or any other appendages. Thus, a pattern like the Brassie, when aligned to, for instance, a Hare's Ear, can cover so much of subsurface food in general terms. This simple pattern can look like a midge pupa (*chironomid*), the intended caddis, even a very impressionistic mayfly nymph. Patterns like this are our saviors and do a lot to make life at the waterside bearable. We have enough trouble trying to cast, figure out trout lies, the creatures that fish eat, the stages of those bugs, to not give ourselves any more unknowables. Simplicity is best here.

An awesome brown trout comes to the waiting net, fooled by a Brassie fished upstream on a spring creek.

TACKLE

As you can imagine, given the variety of waters you can fish with this pattern, the range of tackle can be equally varied. I would, though, suggest that you use a fine tippet in order to assist the sink rate and cut through the water column. This is a very good pattern to put on the "point" position if you are fishing a three-fly Czech nymph team. It seems to be appropriate when seeking out the microcurrents and undulations along the riverbed.

VARIATIONS

By changing the color of the wire and thorax you can summon up a whole galaxy of change and variety. Also, if you add a bead, tungsten or not, your box will offer you an even greater range and depth of opportunities.

EDMONDS & LEE

Season: Early to late
spring, then fall
Type of fish: Trout and grayling

BLACK MAGIC

There has been a rebirth in interest regarding the wet fly, or soft hackle, which is a good thing. This entire group of patterns recalls a time of great men, wild rivers, and a true sense of angling adventure. That these patterns still exist and are as effective as when they were conceived is a testament to the brilliance of those anglers in understanding the ways of trout, food, and fishing.

DIFFICULTY 3/10

MAKING THE FLY

1 Start the well-waxed thread at the eye, making three or four touching-turn securing wraps.

2 Tie in the hackle by the tip. The correct position is important, because it will ultimately affect the entire balance and proportions of the fly—and make the tying of it far simpler.

3 Make very careful touching turns of thread over the hackle tip—this will form the body, too.

4 Take the thread to a point where the hackle tip was tied in. Always make one turn of thread do the job of several—hence the waxing process to add grip and structure to your movements.

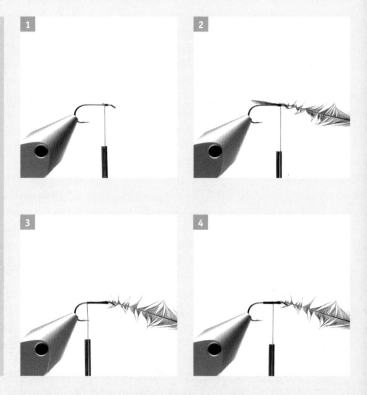

The Black Magic is typical of this genre. Originally it was designed to suggest the pupa of a number of stonefly species, but the fusion of colors could just as well suggest emerging caddis or drowned blue-winged olive spinners—actually, almost anything aquatic. What prevails beyond the actual pattern is how it is fished. Long rods (10–11 ft [3–3.3 m]), light lines (#3–4), high rod tip drifts, and a section of the right type of water. This is crucial: you need riffly broken water runs about knee deep—the kind found just after pools and obstructions. The ideal rivers are tailwaters, such as the Madison and White, to name but two.

Hook: Lightweight wet or dry fly 12–16
Thread: Black, well waxed
Rib: Fine gold wire (optional—the original had none)
Thorax: Peacock herl
Hackle: Black hen

MATERIALS

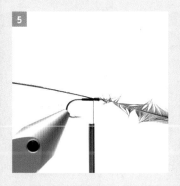
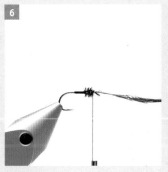

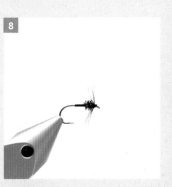

5 Trap in one strand of peacock herl in the thoracic area just at the point where the hackle tip stops. This will give you a very slight thoracic swelling.

6 Wind the strand of herl in very close and abutting turns to a point just short of the eye and where the hackle is to be wound.

7 Wind the hackle so that it "sweeps" back along the hook shank in a way that is similar to a slightly curved open umbrella.

8 Whip finish by making two or three wraps with either the whip finish tool or your hands. If you have waxed the thread correctly, you will only need a minimal number of turns for maximum security.

TACTICS

This whole area of fly design is synonymous with the style of fishing that grew up in the North of England and the upper Clyde area of Scotland. The idea was to fish three flies, with the heaviest at the point, medium in the middle, and the lightest near the surface. As a drowned terrestrial, this fly—and others in the genre—can also be fished upstream as a quasi dry fly. It is also good on stillwaters, mimicking many *chironomid* species.

BEHAVIOR

This fly is about movement. The pulse of hackle in the surface or amid the water layers gives the impression of an envelope of life around the thoracic area—hatching or crushed wings. The essential fish-attracting movement is there, albeit in a micro form. Never fall into the trap of thinking that because it is a "wisp" of a fly it will neither be seen by nor deceive trout. Just think of all the times that you have found trout and other fish—often big ones—eating tiny little black things. I rest my case.

The slim shape looks like many insects—especially midges

This hackle shows the fly "at rest"

When fished or "swung" across the current the hackle folds over the body like a tear drop

TACKLE

This is about using long leaders and light lines on long fly rods. I would consider a 10 ft (3 m) rod taking a #4 floating line as my mainstay on rivers; and often a leader about 12–15 ft (3.6–4.5 m) long. This will allow for the patterns to move in the current, having been cast slightly up and across and allowed to sweep around with the speed of the water. The long rod is to maintain the vital height of the tip to create the acute two-sided triangle with the line that this movement requires.

VARIATIONS

- Try adding a very fine pearly rib.
- Alternatively, try gold, silver, or copper wire.
- You might even change the thorax material to seal's fur (sub).

RIVER RELIABLES
AT THE SURFACE

WILLIAM AUSTEN

Season: *Spring, summer, and even late fall*
Type of fish: *Trout*

BEACON BEIGE

This English West Country pattern from William Austen has always enjoyed mixed fortunes, and it wasn't until the famous British fly tier Peter Deane popularized it in the late 1960s and '70s that people really grasped how good the pattern was—is—when imitating a variety of mayfly species. To this day it is the quintessence of a chalk stream/spring creek pattern: light, sparsely dressed, and representative of a wide number of smaller mayfly species in their adult form—the dun.

DIFFICULTY 6/10

MAKING THE FLY

1 Cover a suitable hook with a layer of thread and then tie in the two hackles at the eye, running the thread down the stripped stalks in touching turns.

2 Trim the thicker ends, then ensure that a layer of thread covers the area and forms a neat taper.

3 Add the tailing material into the gap left by the trimmed hackle stalks. The work you do to make the body layer smooth at this stage will pay dividends when you wind the quill.

4 Tie in a stripped peacock quill. Soaking the quill then softens it and makes it more usable.

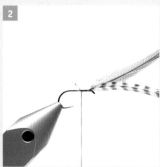

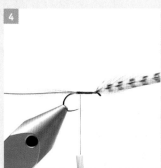

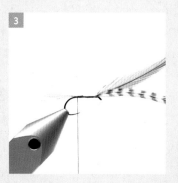

For me, it is the quintessential general-purpose dry fly—the Brassie or Pheasant Tail nymph of the floating world and it can be used whenever you need to generate the impression of mayflies at the surface. Sadly, it has been superseded by a host of new-wave designs incorporating Cul de canard (CDC). This has tended to mask the effectiveness of fully hackled patterns, especially on breezy days when the "footprints" made by the hackle tips in the surface film can well represent the indentations of a natural's feet and be a beacon to the trout. It is still a great pattern to carry and use, and one not to be forgotten on the waters it was designed for: the buoyant little chuckling streams of rain-fed origins.

Hook: Dry fly 14–18, with 16 being the most useful
Thread: Primrose 8/0
Hackle: 1 natural red and 1 grizzly cock hackle wound together
Tail: Mixed fibers of the same
Body: Stripped peacock quill

MATERIALS

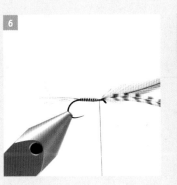

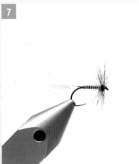

5 Wind the quill in neat abutting turns so that the dark band on the quill nestles into the light to produce a very defined segmented appearance.

6 Coat the quill with either instant glue or nail varnish and allow it to set perfectly hard. This can take anything up to 24 hours, so I tend to "tie off" at this stage. Do a batch of flies up to this point and then let them dry.

7 Wind the hackle in the conventional way. I tend to wind the grizzly first, then wind the natural brown hackle through it and tie off. Make sure the hackles have the same depth of fiber.

8 A quill design of the "old school." While it might seem a radical departure, this CDC pattern uses a quill from a biot, wound in a similar way, but giving a slightly softer, more textured feel. A good variation.

TACTICS

This style of dry fly is ideal for use on fast yet smooth water. I know that sounds contradictory, but if you think about it it's not. You will know the water: streams and freestone rivers that, while containing a maze of riffles, often have their quieter moments, as the water coils around tree trunks and boulders. There, trout hunt at hints of surface life, but do have a little more time to decide on the authenticity of that food than in the riffle and run sections. Enter this pattern—cast upstream using a reasonably short line dropped into likely pockets and areas of observed activity. I have often been known to trim the underside and create an immediate semi-parachute "alternative" spinner pattern; it has gotten me out of a tricky situation on more than one occasion.

Keeping a low profile and casting upstream to a freestone trout feeding on olives—a case for the Beacon Beige.

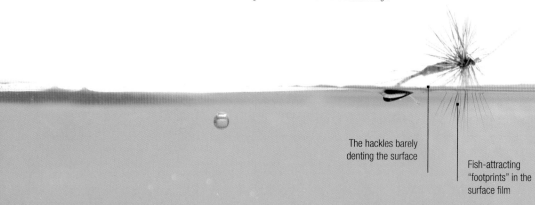

The hackles barely
denting the surface

Fish-attracting
"footprints" in the
surface film

BEHAVIOR

Although, as I have mentioned, it is often ousted in favor of the current crop of CDC, parachutes, and similar "no hackle" concepts, hackle has a very definite role to play—if only as an attraction. First, a hackle resting on the surface film will leave dents or footprints, which is exactly what a natural fly does. It must offer some sort of visual signpost to the fish; actually, we know that it does. Then there is the overall aspect of the pattern: it does actually look as though a natural fly is about to take to the air after having just dried its wings. The trout know that a potential meal might get away. It does not take a genius to figure out what the reaction might be in a food-sparse environment.

A magnificent River Test (U.K.) brown trout is gently cradled before being slipped back into the river that gave us the codification of the classic style of upstream dry fly fishing.

TACKLE

Once again I prefer my 10 ft (3 m) #4 rod and floating line and long leader, but I realize that if you are fishing the smaller streams you must choose your fly rod accordingly. I do use short rods, but still have the lighter lines—and always use as long a leader as I can get away with. On a small stream this might only be 8 ft (2.4 m) but that's better than 7 ft 6 in (2.2 m)!

VARIATIONS

If you add wings (*see the Black Gnat on page 76*) to this pattern you get the classic "quill series": Ginger Quill, Olive Quill, Red Quill, Orange Quill, etc.

LEE WULFF

Season: *Any*
Type of fish: *Trout—all types, grayling, and the occasional salmon*

ROYAL WULFF

This pattern gives me a complete sense of fly-dressing joy to tie. It is just one of those patterns that delights the eye—and, in the role of an attractor dry fly, it is utterly unsurpassed, in my humble opinion. I guess that I could just as easily have selected a Gray, White, or Ausable Wulff. They all work wonderfully, but this version is one I turn to when I need a fly that will drag a fish's attention to the surface. It has turned the heads of a significant number of trout in a vast variety of water types across the globe.

DIFFICULTY 8/10

MAKING THE FLY

1 Tap 30 to 40 fibers of wing hair in a hair stacker and offer this up. Ensure the tips of the hair are offered up in the way they are to be tied in; in this instance, brought up to the hook and then tied in with the tips facing over the eye. Taper the cut of the base fibers at an angle to minimize the dropdown and maintain a smooth taper (also called a "step-cut").

2 Divide the wing into equal halves. Separate by crossing the thread turns, circling the thread around each wing base. Lock the wing in an upright position by securing around the thicker step-cut butts.

3 Tap six to eight moose hock fibers into alignment and tie in immediately after the wing. Step-cut to maintain a smooth body taper and reduce bulk.

4 Make further thread wraps so that you have a smooth taper to work on.

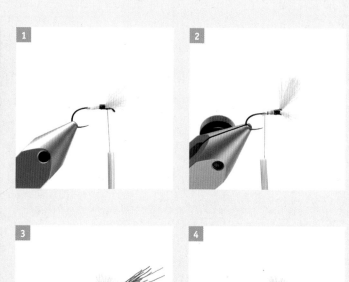

On balance, the place to fish this pattern is on the rougher water associated with boisterous freestone rivers, but I have found it to be very successful for trout on stillwaters, too. The Royal Wulff has also taken a good number of grayling in the smaller sizes, but I would soften the tail a little, as the mouths of grayling tend not to like the abrasive harshness of moose mane. Always carry this one and use it when nothing appears to be moving on the surface.

Hook: Standard dry 8–18

Thread: Black 8/0

Wing: White calf body hair in larger sizes, white polypropylene in smaller

Hackle: Natural red (deep) cock hackle

Tail: Moose mane/hock fibers

Body: First third, peacock herl; second third, red floss (I prefer fluorescent); last third, peacock herl

MATERIALS

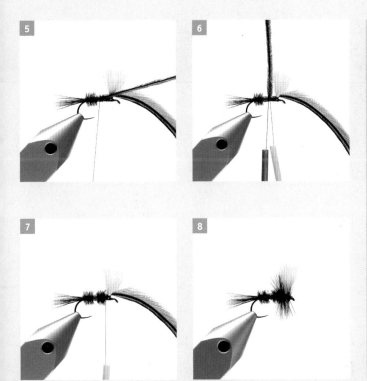

5 Tie in, by the tip, a strand of peacock herl taken from just below the eye and wrap the first third of the body. Also add at this point the hackle. I favor a fairly short-fibered saddle hackle for this. The depth of the hackle fiber should not exceed the point of the hook.

6 Double some red floss around the thread and add this, winding a waist in the middle to form a small hump. Then add a further strand of the peacock herl.

7 Make a further segment of wound peacock herl and tie off.

8 Wind the hackle from the rear of the wing, advancing it forward through the wing in touching turns toward the eye of the hook, and then tie off.

Mauro Mazzo fishes the type of water that was just made for a dry Royal Wulff. It is in this fast water that the shape and color of the design seems to be able to "pull" fish from the depths.

TACTICS

Identifying this fly as a favorite also allows me to tell you about a favorite style of fishing, not purely with this pattern but with almost any buoyant design. Known as the "hopper dropper," the style incorporates a short length (from as short as 4–6 in [10–15 cm] to 18 in [46 cm] or more) of tippet attached to the bend of the dry-fly hook and a small nymph attached to this length: a Pheasant Tail or Mary-Rambo in 16 or 18 is perfect. Supported by the dry fly, this is allowed to drift with it just under the river current at the surface. The virtue of this technique is that the bulk of the dry fly and—in the case of the Royal Wulff—the color scheme attract the fish to the surface, but it often doesn't make the surface assault, because it falls for the deadly little package hanging below. The fly sliding under the water alerts the fisher to the trout's acceptance.

The shape and color is attractive and visible in fast, broken water

The white wing is easy to see over a variety of backgrounds

BEHAVIOR

This is one of those occasions where tactics and behavior meld together. As far as I am aware, there is nothing in nature that looks even vaguely like a Royal Wulff. So what is the attraction? Well, that's just the point—it is an attractor. The color alone seems to hold a fascination for the quarry. I guess it could look a little like an ant or a beetle, but that's stretching the imagination. So what, then? I don't know, but it is clear that the combination of red and peacock colors often proves attractive, so if that works, let's just give it to the trout in abundance—as is the case here. Incidentally, I recall catching the same brown trout three times in one day on the same Royal Wulff, which says a great deal for catch and release, a lot for the fly, but I am not sure about the "gray matter" of the trout concerned.

Rainbow trout of this caliber seem to be attracted to the bright nature of the Royal Wulff, but it does work considerably well for brown trout, too.

TACKLE
Because of the type of water in which a fly like this is often fished—also the often inclement windy conditions that greet the angler on Western waters and other extreme areas—it is probably advisable to use #5 weight rods in either 9 ft (2.7 m) or 10 ft (3 m) and shorter leaders—9 ft (2.7 m) with a very steep profile in order to turn over the bulk of the design.

VARIATIONS
Gray Wulff, Ausable Wulff, and White Wulff

AL TROTH

Season: All—when caddis are
seen on the water
Type of fish: All trout, steelhead,
grayling, and occasionally salmon

ELK HAIR CADDIS

This pattern, I guess, is the "natural imitating" version of
the Royal Wulff, a design that seems to strike a chord with
game fish the globe over. Curiously, while it has caught me
a great many fish on the little, hidden streams of England's
West Country, in places such as Devon and Cornwall, where
there is an abundance of tigerish trout, it seems to do even
better for others.

DIFFICULTY 6/10

MAKING THE FLY

1 Start with the hook in the vise and
attach the primrose thread. This color
is used to blend with the elk hair,
making the head area seem neat and
compact as opposed to contrasted.

2 Run the thread in touching turns
down the hook shank.

3 Having attached a rib (if you want
little weight, choose nylon; if you
want a "glint," choose gold wire),
dub the body with soft animal fur
or polypropylene.

4 Attach the cock hackle in the area
shown, leaving ample room to tie in
the wing, which is bulky.

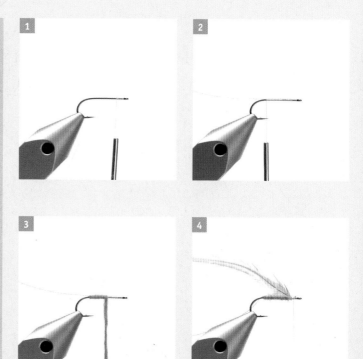

In any fast-water situation when caddis are flitting about, this is a first-choice pattern, but in smoother flows and stillwaters it should be augmented by a slightly more realistically profiled pattern, such as the Envelope Caddis/Sedge. In fact, you can adapt this pattern by putting some CDC underneath the elk hair wing to get a variant known as Skippy's Sedge. This fly, though, is testament to Al Troth, to the legendary Montana guide's genius of observation and his ability to take an abundant material and fashion it into one of the world's best-loved caddis patterns. Try it, too, on stillwaters when a small wake "attractor" pattern is required to entice fish to home in on the surface; in this role it will seldom disappoint you.

Hook: Standard dry fly 8–18
Thread: Primrose or tan 8/0
Rib: Fine gold wire or nylon mono
Body: Soft animal fur dubbing (possum under-fur, rabbit, etc.), color to match intended species
Hackle: Palmered ginger cree, natural red or grizzly cock hackle
Wing: Cow or yearling elk hair combed and tapped into alignment

MATERIALS

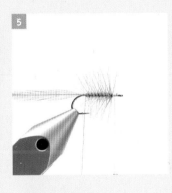

5

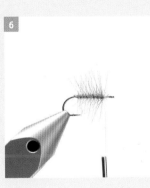

6

7

8

5 Palmer the hackle as shown, in even turns, ensuring the fibers spiral consistently and do not get caught up in one another.

6 Rib through the hackle with an almost rocking motion of the rib so as not to trap precious hackle barbules.

7 Prepare the elk hair wing by stroking out the under-fur with a pet comb prior to tapping in alignment with a hair-stacking device (see page 10). Don't overdo the hair, but do get rid of the under-fur, or you will have an insecure wing.

8 Tie in the wing by taking the hair out of the stacker in the direction you want it to project along the shank. Take the wraps firmly at first, but build on the tension so that you get minimum flare. Trim the butts flush with the hook eye.

TACTICS

There isn't much more to say about fishing this pattern other than, "Do it!" I have yet to come across a better search pattern in a variety of water types. Admittedly, you might argue that there are better patterns for fishing really fast water, in low light, and so on, but when you consider that this fly is equally at home on still, running, fast, or slow water, then its use to the fisher is all-embracing. You can use it moving or static. The situation will determine the method—just make sure that you have some in the size and color of your hatch.

A young Czech fly fisher uses the Elk Hair Caddis on the top dropper to deadly effect in pocket water.

The fly can be almost danced across the surface

The hackle and wing provide the buoyancy for a wide range of situations

BEHAVIOR

Given that this fly does imitate a caddis, knowing something about the natural's lifestyle is important. Caddis tend to be an afternoon hatching species, and they can drift quite a long way before hatching. Once hatched on the surface, many caddis make an identifiable scurrying motion along the surface to the sanctuary of the bank or into the sky, depending on the species. This pattern's silhouette and buoyancy emulates this, and the creature's habits are a clue as to how and where to fish it. But it can be fished at rest, too. You see what I mean by versatile? There is one other stage left to the fly fisher. It is when the female shoots under the surface to lay her eggs. This diving caddis stage has been imitated with specific patterns, but a sunk Elk Hair Caddis can be very effective.

An adult caddis (in this case, the U.K. Cinnamon Sedge, Limnephilus rhombicus) is typical of most adult species, and by having a pattern like the Elk Hair, a vast group of natural fly hatches can be catered to with one style of pattern, merely by changing the body color and size.

TACKLE

You can choose more or less whatever you prefer here, although I favor the longer rod. A 10 ft (3 m) #4 or #5 is perfect, because you can get the elevation to skitter the fly along the surface in a lifelike manner. A floating line is needed, of course, and a reasonably long leader where appropriate.

VARIATIONS

There have been many variations based on this theme—some with sculpted "muddler" heads, others with CDC underwings, and so on, but all tend to conform to this basic design. Natural and bleached elk are the mainstays, but try others if the hatches warrant it.

GEORGE HALLADAY

Season: All
Type of fish: Trout and grayling

ADAMS (PARACHUTE)

The world's most used and popular dry fly? Probably. I know of few fly fishers who would not place this indispensable design in their top ten. I also know of few trout that will refuse its subtle charms when presented correctly. Think of a situation and use this pattern. Regardless of whether you are trying to unravel a complex hatch and need something familiar to hang a metaphorical hat on, or you need a fly that is a vague impression of a whole host of surface-born creatures, this is the fly that can unlock doors.

DIFFICULTY 6/10

MAKING THE FLY

1 For this particular parachute "post," align some calf body hair and tie it in with the tips facing over the hook eye. Note: Ensure that you tie this in on top of a thread base.

2 Raise the forward-facing fibers up and then make successive turns of thread at the base of the post to ensure it stands nearly upright. Trim the rear in a staggered, tapering cut and cover this with thread.

3 Tie in the two hackles and then take the thread around the post to create a firm base of thread to rotate the hackles on. Take the wraps up the post sufficiently far to ensure the hackles have enough "depth" to craft the right amount of fiber flare around the post.

4 Return the thread to the usual place on the hook shank. Tie in a mixed fiber tail.

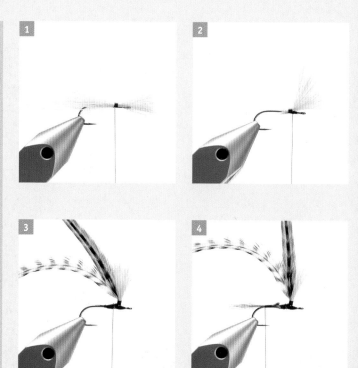

This is simply one of those patterns that covers most of the up-winged species reasonably well and, I am told, started life in its fully hackled form as a caddis imitation. It is also a truly awesome stillwater design. Well, that just about covers every fly-fishing situation, so why fish with anything else? Of course there would be no fun in just carrying one style of dry fly in a variety of sizes, but it's a thought for those fly fishers who are first venturing into the sport and need a pattern in which they can place all their confidence. This is the one.

Hook: Standard dry (10) 12–22
Thread: Black 8/0–12/0
Wing: White calf body hair tied as a post (or polypropylene)
Hackle: Natural red-brown and grizzly cock hackle mixed
Tail: Fibers of the same
Body: Gray under-fur from rabbit, possum, muskrat, beaver, etc.

MATERIALS

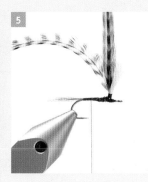

5 Dub the body with fur. I use a noodle dub to ensure that I get a nice neat segmentation to the body to mirror the natural.

6 Invert the fly and make sure that you dub around the post. If you do not turn the fly upside down there can be a gap and an ugliness to the fly at this point.

7 Now wind the grizzly hackle down the post in close turns and secure at the thorax, followed by the natural red hackle. It is important to then secure the hackles at the thorax area, having first built up a "shoulder" of dubbing.

8 Finish by adding a little more dubbing toward the eye.

TACTICS

Given the general nature of the design, it is difficult to identify a specific role for this fly, tactically. That, actually, is not the role for the fly, as you will already have figured out; but by having a pattern like this, and then (within the basic design) growing a range of sizes, you can concentrate on the actual fishing. I have lost count of the times I have seen anglers burrow into their many and various boxes with knitted brows, trying to come up with a solution to the problems on the water in front of them. Faced by a sea of choices, confusion floods in like a tide. So with just a couple of designs to cover the overall size, shape, and aspect, you can meet the trout's surface demands head on—and generally win.

A rainbow trout in shallow, smooth water is a hard taskmaster for presentation. An Adams is perfect, because of the soft descent and delicate hackle footprints on the surface, so similar to the natural's foot marks.

The fly on touchdown prior to settling

The parachute hackle lets the fly sit low on the surface

BEHAVIOR

As I have suggested, this design is made to grip the surface and ride the water "low." The reason for this is that natural flies in the process of hatching have to burst through the considerable barrier that the surface tension presents (the task has been likened to a human trying to push through four feet (1.3 m) of earth to reach air), and they then rest after their exertions. The way the parachute supports the fly represents this aspect exceptionally well. It might pay you to carry both the conventional fully winged and hackled version, as well as this parachute version. Doing so will simulate species hatching on a windy day, adults (caddis and mayflies) about to alight from the water (the full-hackled version), naturals trapped in the surface on calm days, or their general surface development.

With light failing on this English chalk stream flies come out to play. An Adams, due to its general appeal, can cover both the Dun and the spinner stages.

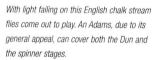

TACKLE

The issue of tackle is a difficult one, for this is truly a fly for all occasions and all eventualities. I guess if I were restricted to one outfit, I would opt for a #4 line and a rod that meets the water's criteria—9 ft (2.7 m) or 10 ft (3 m) for big rivers (and stillwaters) and 7 ft or 8 ft (2.1 or 2.4 m) for smaller streams. Always match the tippet to the fly size and use as long a leader as you feel you can get away with.

VARIATIONS

By varying the color of the calf hair wing you can meet the demands of some very awkward light conditions and, crucially, maintain the sight of your pattern. If you are having difficulty tying in the "bulk" of the hair you might find Antron far easier (*see the Glitter [AKA Twinkle] Gulper dressing, page 180*). Whatever you do, don't forget the original!

KLINKHAMMER

I know what I might have said about the Adams'
effectiveness, but ask most European river fishers and this
pattern will be right up there, too. Created one evening by
the two "greats" of European fly tying, the late Hans de
Groot and Hans van Klinken, the latter has since gone on to
craft this pattern into one that I simply would not want to be
without, in any river situation, fast, slow, or in between.

HANS VAN KLINKEN & HANS DE GROOT

Season: All
Type of fish: *Grayling and trout*

DIFFICULTY 7/10

MAKING THE FLY

1 Add a layer of thread on the
hook and offer up a strand of dense
polypropylene. Tie this in directly on
top of the hook with touching turns of
thread at the midpoint of the thoracic
area of the shaped hook.

2 Add the hackle. Make sure you use a
good dry fly quality that is long. Create
the post by crossing the thread around
the base so that it stands upright.

3 Swing the thread around the base
of the post and then secure the
stripped hackle stalk to it. Take turns
up the post, binding the hackle and
strengthening the post. The number of
turns will determine the revolutions
of hackle downward.

4 Run the thread to beyond the bend
of the hook. Add a strand of dubbing
to form a tapering noodle and march
this in touching turns up the shank.

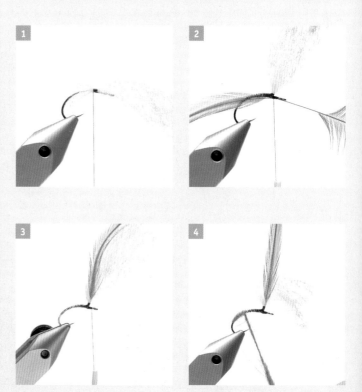

Originally designed to represent a hatching sedge specifically for European grayling (which have a very particular way of sipping a dry fly from the surface, given their mouth shape with a longer upper lip), this fly has since proved deadly for trout in all waters. The design is challenging to tie, but do not take short cuts—I have tried and the effect is not as good. Stay pattern specific. Oddly, it is a pattern that has never really caught on in the U.S. The angler's loss is the trout's gain!

Hook: TMC 200 or Klinkhammer special hook (Partridge) 8–18

Thread: Claret or black 8/0

Wing: White polypropylene tied as a post

Hackle: Natural red cock hackle (or Greenwell)

Body: Tan, gray, pale yellow, olive, etc. Poly dubbing

Thorax: Peacock herl

MATERIALS

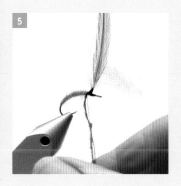

5 Dub until the hook takes a different shape. Add the strand of peacock herl. (I turn this, too, into a dubbing rope for strength and extra "fuzz.")

6 Wind this strand through the thorax. This job will be made a great deal easier—as will the procedures for the rest of the fly—if you tilt the fly and rotate the vise to one side on a horizontal plane.

7 Cover the thorax with the peacock herl, ensuring that there are no gaps. Finish by tying off around the post.

8 Wind the hackle down to the thorax in as many revolutions as you think the job, or the water to be fished, will require. Be careful to run down the post in almost touching turns: never cross over with a parachute hackle. Whip finish around the base of the post.

Josh Day leads a Klinkhammer, holding a smaller-weighted nymph through a lovely glide of water on the Fisherman's Paradise section of Penn States' spring creek.

TACTICS

OK—duo and trio fishing. To the fly line, attach a plaited, standard, or braided leader of about 5 ft (1.5 m), tapering to a nylon tippet section of 5X. This can slightly longer than the braid, so that the length from fly line to fly is about 6–7 ft (1.8–2.1 m). Attach the Beast or Klinkhammer to the tippet conventionally, then attach a further length of tippet to the bend of the hook. The length will be determined by the depth of the water, as will the use of either one or two patterns below. The deeper the water, the longer the nylon lengths below the dry fly. In shallow water, attach a second fly to this length of nylon. In deeper water, add an 18 in–3 ft (0.5–0.9 m) section of 5–6X nylon, then a further (often longer) section of tippet (in similar diameter) via a water knot. Place two patterns below the dry fly, one on the dropper, one on the point—and now search the water.

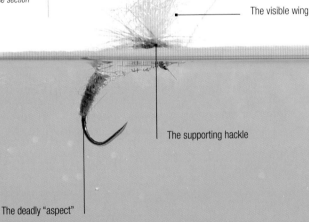

The visible wing

The supporting hackle

The deadly "aspect"

BEHAVIOR

Because this pattern was originally designed to meet a very specific phase in the caddis lifecycle, it would seem appropriate to look at this area, knowing of course that it remains one of the best natural "attractor" dry flies in existence. There are not many vulnerable stages in the caddis lifecycle: caddis are quick in the water column and almost uniquely camouflaged when in the larval state. However, when they are about to venture into adulthood at the surface, and are caught between the stages of pupa and adult, they are vulnerable and almost at the mercy of the trout—and grayling—as they drift inert on the surface. Enter the Klinkhammer.

A South Fork Snake River cutthroat slides back having just accepted a Klinkhammer in pocket water. Trout don't understand geography!

TACKLE
This is a tough one, because this fly is fairly tackle insensitive. I would, though, having made a case for the duo and trio, suggest that this style be used on a 10 ft (3 m) #4 or #5 rod. A floating line is needed, of course—even if you won't be using much of it.

VARIATIONS
Foam can be used to create the post, and CDC also works well. Varying the body colors will give you a wonderful range of permutations.

SPARKLE GNAT

I am not sure when I first came across the Griffiths Gnat. I don't doubt that it was a massive inspiration, and it has remained a key pattern down the years. However, I did feel it lacked just a little something, so I decided to experiment and see what I could do about it.

CHARLES JARDINE VIA RANDALL KAUFMANN & OTHERS

Season: All
Type of fish: Trout and grayling, and also panfish

DIFFICULTY 3/10

MAKING THE FLY

1 Offer up the thread and attach at the eye. Then almost immediately work in a white CDC feather (or two feathers for larger sizes) with the tip tied "advanced," i.e., facing forward. As with the "F" Fly (*see page 80*), with finger and thumb pressure pull the stem to reduce and condense.

2 Tie in the Twinkle strands for the tail, and in touching turns run the thread to the eye.

3 Strip a section of the hackle free of fiber. Run this stem the length of the shank, stopping short of the eye to eliminate lumps or bumps. Choose a saddle hackle as opposed to a neck hackle, because saddle hackles are more even in their taper along the stem.

4 Add the peacock herl strand.

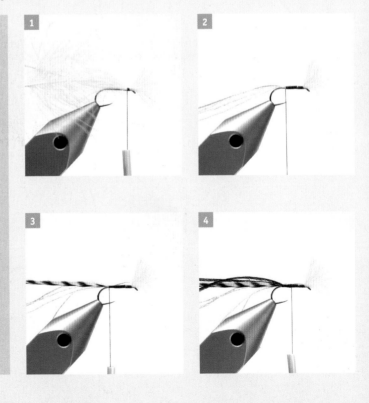

Back around the early '90s I decided to add a strand or two of reflective material—Twinkle (Crystal Hair works as well). This seemed to improve the pattern a lot, and the success that the original enjoyed was further enhanced by incorporating the very visual white CDC, which is great for spotting a tiny fly in less-than-good visibility. Now this pattern is my first choice in almost any small-fly situation, be it still or running water. I can't think of many patterns that are either as versatile or as geographically embracing as this one. My advice is: just carry it!

Hook: TMC 103 BL or light wire dry fly equivalent 15–21 (16–20)

Thread: Black, claret 12/0 or clear spider web

Tail: 2 strands of Twinkle or Crystal Hair (in orange, pearl, black, olive, etc.)

Wing: 1–2 white CDC hackle tips

Hackle: Grizzly cock spade/saddle hackle

Rib: 4X mono (optional and only used if palmered in the "classic" manner)

Body: 1–2 strands of peacock herl

MATERIALS

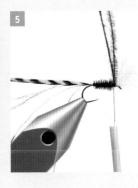

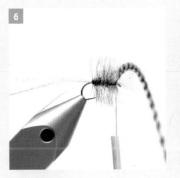

5 Wind the peacock herl to the point where the wing was tied and ensure that the wing stands vertical from the shank with thread wraps both fore and aft.

6 Palmer the hackle up the herl-covered body and tie in either immediately behind or in front of the wing. I try to mirror the turns of peacock herl to some extent with the turns of hackle so it looks as though there is a "ruff" of peacock herl peeking from beneath the hackle fibers. The body should look even and "fuzzy."

7 The finished fly for broken water.

8 In smoother flows and ultra midge situations, trim the underside in a "V" against the natural rotation of the fiber. This way the fibers will be even on both sides.

A rainbow warrior taken by a Sparkle Gnat, just as evening descended on an eastern U.S. spring creek—a time when very often the small fly out-fishes the larger.

TACTICS

It is difficult to pin down just one tactic for a pattern that enjoys such a wide range of uses and styles of fishing, but one of the key things with this design is that the wing—the white CDC—really makes it stand out in a confused current flow and a variety of backdrops and light sources. This makes the "Gnat" very useful for fishing a small pattern in areas of the stream with difficult lighting—back eddies, under trees, and even in bright light—or when fishing a small fly at longer range, which is always a nightmare. The other great thing is that because of its size and shape, it tends not to set the alarm bells ringing in the quarry's suspicious mind.

The flotation and visibility of CDC

The footprint of hackle

The glint in the tail

BEHAVIOR

This is really a "fuzzy" Black Gnat, but the idea behind the original Griffiths Gnat was to try to convey a whole mass of tiny *chironomids* forming into tiny clusters and rolling about the surface. Not unrealistically—please excuse the term—these are known as "balling midges." This aspect of behavior seems to occur through the colder months on waters like the Bighorn, Madison, and other midge-inhabited rivers of the West, though I am sure it happens elsewhere; I certainly know it happens on rivers in Central Wales and in the North of England.

Trico-Spinners caught in nature's trap: a cobweb. When just about to start a day or evening by a stream, have a quick glance at these natural fly collectors. That way you will have a very good idea what is hatching on the stream, which will then affect your fly choice.

TACKLE

Again (sorry to be boring about this), the usual 10 ft (3 m) #4 is the way to go—shorter if you must, but you should always try to use as long a fly rod as you can get away with for the task, and long leaders too.

VARIATIONS

None, apart from changing the color of the tail to match the hatch.

FREDERIC HALFORD & OTHERS

Season: *All, but primarily late spring to early fall*
Type of fish: *Trout and grayling*

BLACK GNAT

"Little black numbers" abound in fly fishing, and this is just one of a plethora that you could choose from—one, furthermore, that has been with us for a very long time. So why, then, ignore the modern in favor of the ancient? Sentiment, for one thing—and, of course, the fact that it still works just fine.

DIFFICULTY 7/10

MAKING THE FLY

1 Tie in a black cock hackle on top of a layer of thread at the thorax.

2 Pair two mallard secondary quill fibers and "soft loop" these in using the "pinch and loop" style of winging incorporating well-waxed thread. (*See page 17 for detail of this procedure.*)

3 Wind a quill body (*see the Beacon Beige on page 52*), tie off immediately behind the wing, and then wind the hackle through the wing.

4 Alternatively, add a layer of thread and then the hackle—a soft henny cock hackle is the way to go here.

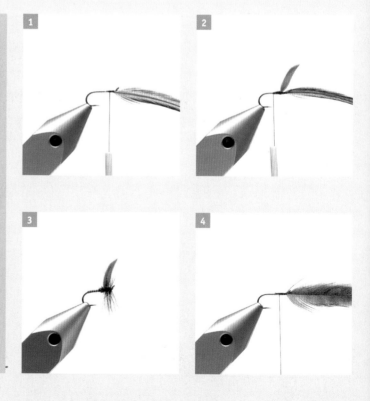

This pattern also allows me to bring to the table a sense of our history. So often the patterns that were crafted a century ago are considered obsolete, out of date, and worthless, but trout—indeed, fish in general—have no idea of history, and if a pattern worked back then, why not now? This pattern recalls times of "smutting" on English chalk streams—not a dubious activity, but a time when trout selectively feed on tiny black *Diptera* flies and become very difficult to catch indeed. This pattern was conceived for just such an occasion by one of the father figures of the dry fly, and it still works well to this day.

Hook: Up-eyed dry fly 16–20
Thread: Black 12/0 (well waxed)
Hackle: Black henny cock hackle
Body: Stripped peacock quill
Wing: Paired Mallard Primary quill (upright) or blue dun cock hackle points (flat)
Thorax: Optional—dyed black mole

MATERIALS

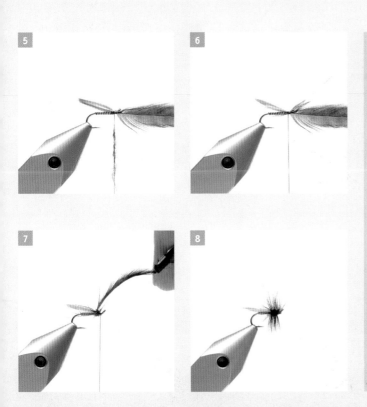

5 Take the thread to the hook bend and secure it. Then wind a strand of natural quill (as in the Beacon Beige) up to the thorax. Now, with the same secondary mallard quill slips, place them concave tip to concave tip in order to create the reverse of the split dry fly wing but now a wet fly wing. Pinch and loop this on top of the shank so that it slopes back to the bend.

6 Now add a very small amount of dubbing to the thoracic area, immediately in front of the wing.

7 Wind the hackle in the usual way.

8 The completed Halfordian fly.

High spring, a hint of warmth, and the crystal waters of a chalk stream combine to offer the right opportunities for fishing the Black Gnat.

TACTICS

The Black Gnat works in two different trout situations and one grayling. The first is when the mayfly (*E. danica*) are on the water and, try as you might, with trout rising all around you cannot catch fish. What you may have found is a "masked hatch"—trout looking as though they are taking the obvious when they are actually taking the almost invisible alternative fly. Enter the Black Gnat. The second occurs on those high summer days. Amid the flowing river a trout languidly sips something from the surface. Enter the tiny Black Gnat. In the third case, it's almost winter, the river is littered with fall's debris, and across the surface tiny dark forms grip the surface like pinpricks. Suddenly bubbly rises break the gloom. Enter the grayling... and the Black Gnat.

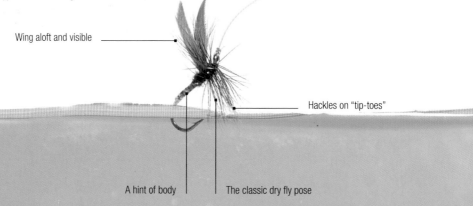

Wing aloft and visible

Hackles on "tip-toes"

A hint of body

The classic dry fly pose

BEHAVIOR

The natural is part of that massive group known as *Diptera*—the true flies—and a member of the subgroup *Bibio johannis*. Of course, to confuse matters further, there are several species of black gnat, but do trout or grayling know this? Probably not. From an angler's perspective, the thing about gnats—black or not—is that they are available to trout (and grayling) over the majority of the season; the fact that they are surface-bound and largely terrestrial means that they can evoke a rise from the fish at any given point and on almost any water type. This is great news for us fishers: all we have to do is to recognize the moment and then get to work.

We might have PVC floating lines and carbon fly rods, but the use and the style—and the fly patterns, too—haven't changed massively since Halford's time. Neither, of course, has the quarry: they don't know the names of fly patterns, nor what year they are living in!

TACKLE

I would go light here, and err on the side of rods taking a #3 or #4 floating line. The other area that I would also look to is leader length, and while you might only be using, for instance, a 7 ft (2.1 m) leader on a small stream, I would add a further lighter tippet of 18 in (0.5 m) to that leader. If I were using a 9 ft (2.7 m) leader I would go up to 10 ft or even 12 ft (3 or 3.6 m). There is no question in my mind that long leaders mean more trout.

VARIATIONS

As depicted in step 8 or step 4, depending on your inclination and the trout's preference.

MARJAN FRATNIK

Season: All
Type of fish: Trout and grayling

"F" FLY

Well, they don't come much simpler or deadlier than this little beauty from Marjan Fratnik. The first I heard about this pattern was from an old friend and noted fly-fishing authority, Taff Price. He had fished in Slovenia with Fratnik and had come back to the U.K. with this deadly concoction of floatability, all-things-to-all-trout, and a huge flat/delta wing silhouette reminiscent of so many caddis and midge species.

DIFFICULTY **4/10**

MAKING THE FLY

1 For this pattern I favor the hook known as the TMC 103 BL, a barbless hook that is light, strong, and fantastic when it comes to hooking grayling. It is a design that just seems to work better than others for this species. It is excellent for trout, too.

2 Offer up the tying thread, make the initial wraps, and take the thread in touching turns to the hook bend. (This is the point that the chosen body material should be tied in.)

3 Now you either return the thread to the thoracic area, creating a simple wound thread body, or you dub, or you wind a CDC feather in by the tip (or other selected body material) along the shank. Your choice.

4 Select two CDC feathers for hook sizes 16 and lower, three for 14, and so on; match these tip to tip.

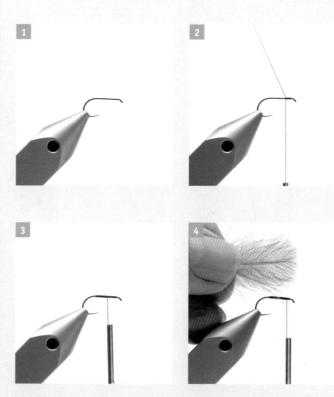

It has worked devastatingly well when trout are feeding "tetchily" in the surface film—quite possibly because it could be mistaken for the "succor" stage, the crippled mayfly dun in its death throes between nymph and adulthood, its demise brought on by the exertions of trying to burst through the surface film. It is another must-have in the box, especially in sizes of 16 and below. It is especially effective on picky grayling just brushing the surface with their noses.

Hook: TMC 103 BL dry fly or similar lightweight hook

Thread: Gray, olive, claret 8/0

Body: Thread, wound CDC (as per original dressing), stripped peacock quill (my favorite), or dubbed CDC

Wing: A cluster (3 or so) of CDC feather tips. That's it: honest!

MATERIALS

5 Now tie the feathers directly on top of the hook shank. This can be much more difficult than it looks, given both the bulk of the feather and its inherently slippery nature.

6 With finger and thumb pressure on the base of the feathers, pull these very gently under the securing wraps to condense the wing and reduce the length. Keep the number of thread wraps to a minimum, but make sure they are secure.

7 Try to achieve a smooth, small, neat head area around the hook eye.

8 The finished result should look something like this.

TACTICS

I think that one could safely say that just about any dry fly style suits this pattern: upstream, across, and (heaven forbid) downstream. The one thing I would urge is accurate, delicate presentation. First you have to figure out whether the fish you are casting to is lying deep or near the surface. The trick is to watch the rise form. If it is languid and lazy, almost like a casual shoulder barge at the surface, then the chances are the fish is sitting high in the water near the surface. If it is almost splashy and outwardly "hurried," then the fish is probably sitting much deeper. You can then adjust your cast and the fly's drift to the fish's last rising position.

BEHAVIOR

Now here is the problem. The "F" Fly was wholly designed to represent something and nothing to a trout or grayling. As Fratnik says, "In my fifty-eight years [more now, I guess] of fly fishing, I have always tried to figure out why a trout takes a certain fly, nymph, or streamer that looks like nothing found on the water. Having found some almost impossible things in trout and grayling stomachs...I convinced myself that these fish will sometimes take anything foodlike..." That says it all.

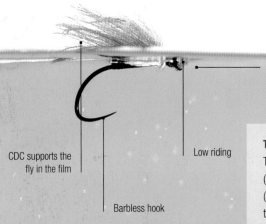

Sunk tippet

CDC supports the
fly in the film

Low riding

Barbless hook

TACKLE
The usual dry fly regalia. I would urge you use the 10 ft (3 m) #4...but then I would, wouldn't I? If you are allowed (and in many parts of North America regulations forbid the use of multiple flies), try using two "F" Flies on the same leader about 3 ft (0.9 m) apart. It works brilliantly.

VARIATIONS
Fratnik now uses a dubbed body rather than the original wound CDC; you can easily vary the color, considering the natural CDC color variations and the dyed feathers that are now available.

THE CUTTING
EDGE BELOW

JIRI KLIMA

Season: Any
Type of fish: Trout, grayling, and some coarse fish

JIRI'S JIG

I will never forget the day. I was giving a streamside lesson where Czech fly fisher and one-time Czech national fly-fishing captain and coach Jiri Klima happened to be. I watched him crank this simple pattern out on his vise, right by the river, tie it on the tip of his three-fly leader (which was only about 8 ft [2.4 m] long!), then wade out into a river he had never seen, and with his first few casts catch some fabulous fish. I wrote an article about him soon after, calling him the "river god." I still stand by that statement.

DIFFICULTY 3/10

MAKING THE FLY

1 Either prepare a hook with a bead or secure a preformed "jig" hook in the vise.

2 Wrap a layer of thread down the shank, stopping halfway down to work in some tailing fibers (five to six is fine); try to select the softer natural red cock hackle fibers rather than the harsher, brittle ones.

3 At the hook bend offer up a strand of the plastic body material and cut a defined angled as shown. Tie this in by the fine tip of the material.

4 Wrap the body in successive layers and secure at the head. Ensure that you firm a neat smooth taper to the body. Add a small contrasting thorax of Ice Dub and you are done.

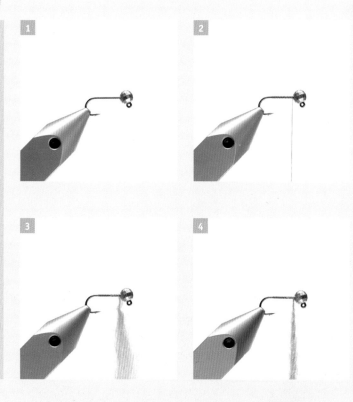

I must admit, I have yet to see a better fish-catching machine or one that reads water so well. It was the simplicity that won me over; the simplicity of both technique and pattern. Just this fly on the point, another slightly lighter one (a small Czech Nymph) about 2 ft (0.6 m) above, and an even lighter pattern 3 ft (0.9 m) above that. If it's shallower water (or if rules only allow two flies), then deduct the upper pattern. Since that time, I have lost count of the fish I have caught on designs like this. And it's so versatile: I have used it with outstanding results throughout the Western rivers of the U.S., the U.K., Slovenia—everywhere. Trout don't have a language or geography barrier, nor do grayling; they just engulf the thing! The best thing is the fact that it is so easy to tie.

Hook: A preformed gold "jig" hook or a gold bead threaded on a similarly shaped hook, 10–16

Thread: 8/0 to match or contrast dramatically with the body, e.g. olive body/olive thread, or amber body/bright red thread

Tail: Natural red cock hackles

Body: Magic Glass Nymph Body, Scud Back, or any thin vinyl-based body material in olive tones; alternatively, use Ice Dub or similar "soft" synthetic Antron-like dubbing in amber, cream, tan, etc.

Hackle: None

MATERIALS

5 The same as step 1, but run the thread (contrasting) to the bend and work in the fibers of the dubbing.

6 Spin the dubbing into a single, intertwined strand: form a rough taper of material by rotating the strands in one direction between your fingers and thumb and knitting the fibers together. Secure these strands at the bead/thoracic area, continuing the spiral without the thread, and rotate around the shank, maintaining tension and maintaining (or adding to) the twisted strand as you wind down the shank.

7 Run the dubbing to the hook bend and secure; strip away any body material and return the thread to the thorax.

8 For this smooth version all you do is add a cock hackle tail and wind two or three layers of Nymph Body, or similar vinyl body material, in an array of olives. The thorax remains the same.

TACTICS

You need water that is going to be flowing fairly quickly and with a depth of between 2 ft and 4 ft (0.6–1.2 m). The concept is to cast this pattern on the point of the leader toward an upstream position, and then let it grip the current and plunge through the surface, taking the cargo of other flies with it. Be aware that you will probably have no fly line out of the tip; this is about measuring the leader and fishing just over the actual depth of water you have selected. The key is to maintain total control and tension in the leader and the flies at all times as they swing down the current from the upstream side and past your in-stream position. The idea is that they end up immediately below you and, driven by the force of water, start to swing up toward the surface.

A perfect riffle and James Hunt, one of the leading young English river fly fishers, stoops to conquer on one of his favorite stretches of the River Wharfe in the U.K.

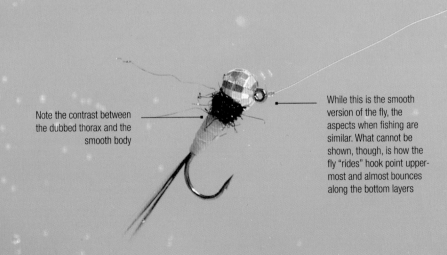

Note the contrast between the dubbed thorax and the smooth body

While this is the smooth version of the fly, the aspects when fishing are similar. What cannot be shown, though, is how the fly "rides" hook point uppermost and almost bounces along the bottom layers

BEHAVIOR

This pattern is not representative of natural flies in the accepted
sense; rather, it is reminiscent of a broad spectrum. The olive
smooth-bodied design could be vaguely suggestive of various mayfly
nymphs, whereas the rough-bodied pattern is closer to a sedge
pupa. But, then, the quarry doesn't know that—they just see the
fly as something that looks like a natural food form in an area
where they expect to find it.

*A small Austrian Tyrol stream is the perfect
water speed and height for using a small Jig.
The neighboring main river, the Traun, was
home during the early '70s to a style of Jig
that Jiri Klima based his design upon.*

TACKLE

I tend to use the 10 ft (3 m) #5 when fishing this design with other flies
on the leader. The leader is the most important aspect, and should be just
under or over the length of the fly rod. You need a single diameter nylon
when using the Czech style—usually 4X–5X Stroft nylon, which is attached
directly to a braided loop in the fly line. On smaller streams, use shorter rods
and match the leader length accordingly.

VARIATIONS

See step by step illustrations: smooth and rough designs.

JIRI KLIMA &
JAN SIMANS

Season: All
Type of fish: Game fish
(all trout, salmon, grayling, plus many other species)

CZECH NYMPH

There are few methods and fly patterns that you can truly call revolutionary. For that to be created you have to change an entire mindset, offer a new vision of something, and then get the process adopted across a broad spectrum of people. The Czech Nymph and the style of fishing that goes with it have done exactly that, altering how we approach and fish sections of rivers where once we only found meager pickings.

DIFFICULTY 4/10

MAKING THE FLY

1 Place a layer of thread along the hook shank. Take a length of lead wire about the same diameter as the hook wire and wind it up the hook shank. Coat this in turn with instant glue to "heal" any micro gaps in the turns.

2 Shape the wire by pressing the sides with a pair of smooth-jawed hemostats so that the lead turns have flat sides and a rounded top and bottom. Place the ribbing material in the gap between the last turn of wire and the last turn of thread around the hook bend.

3 Take a length of dubbing and apply this as in the Jiri's Jig. Use a noodle pre-tapered strand caught in by fibers at the bend then wound up the shank, but in a loose wrap and not one that will take on a noticeable segmentation.

4 Once you are proficient you can blend colors into the twined fibers to create "hot spots" and thoracic changes.

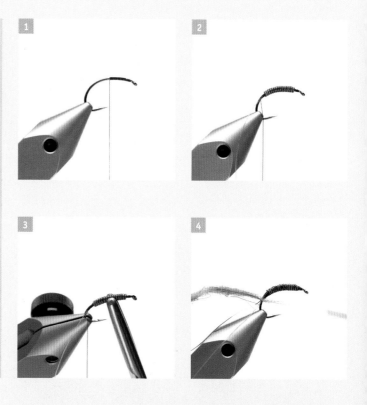

This strategy was devised to catch grayling, often in very fast water. It is a brutally efficient way of searching layers, especially at the bottom, and leaving very little of the water column or any point in the stream uncovered. The fact that trout succumb with greedy alacrity, as well, is all to our benefit. The other great thing about this method is the simplicity of it. It is about brave wading and continuous, almost rhythmic, coverage of sections of the stream. It takes the form of cast, drift, let the flies dig deep, drift, swing up, mandatory little strike, lift, and repeat. That's it. But it is the choice of water, the concentration of the fisher, that little bit of nylon, fly line, and leader, and the way in which the fly is situated on that leader more than the fly itself, on which success depends.

Hook: Lightweight curved grub hook, 6–14

Thread: To match body—I use a great deal of light yellow/naples 8/0

Rib 1: Medium pearl Mylar or gold or silver tinsel

Rib 2: 3–4 lb (1.3–1.8 kg) nylon

Body: Animal fur, softer Antrons, Ice Dub, etc. to produce the color scheme that you require. I mix the materials to suit the task

Shell back: Magic Shrimp foil, Scud Back, or trimmed latex glove (any pharmacy or hardware store will have these) Pantone-penned the correct shade on the underside of the material

MATERIALS

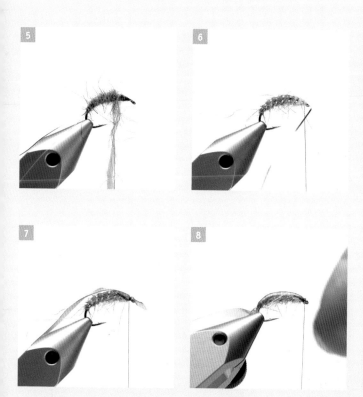

5 Now rib with the Mylar in the same way that you placed the dubbing in order to "bed" it in. You should not exceed five turns: this seems to give the fly balance.

6 Now attach the Magic Shrimp foil with the thread at the head area/hook eye (odd way round, I know, but stay with me here!).

7 Stretch the foil back down the entire back with your finger and thumb and secure at the hook bend with two or three turns of the nylon rib. Run this nylon rib back up the dressing, encompassing both the back and body in fairly close yet very even segments, and finish at the head.

8 Lastly, with a dubbing needle, pick out some dubbing strands in the thoracic area to "hint" at legs.

Young Welsh wizard Shaun Jones fishes the upper Vltava, home to many Czech nymphing styles and just about the most perfect water to use with the style.

TACTICS

The essence of the style lies in the selection of water: a ripple-filled stretch with a good vigorous flow of about 2–6 ft (0.6–1.8 m) depth is ideal. There is some disagreement as to whether you should fish up or downstream. In some water types the cast-and-sweep style upstream works better, but in other areas—especially as you near a pool or dropoff—it pays to fish downstream. It really is a case of casting and letting the leader system—three flies in heavy flows and two in shallower, lighter flows—grip the current and descend. It is important that you maintain control of the leader at all times; so much so that you can lift and drop the flies and actually feel the patterns either "click" the bottom or be enfolded in the tension of the current. Using a single diameter of nylon leader and no fly line heightens this awareness, and some anglers have even used coarse anglers' braided Dynema to enhance this subsurface "feel."

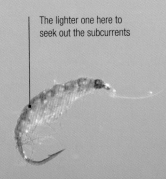

The lighter one here to seek out the subcurrents

BEHAVIOR

This is a difficult one, because the idea of the Czech Nymph was to convey a great deal with a small range of patterns—basically the design was crafted to imitate non-case-making caddis species such as *Rhyacophila*, *Hydropsyche*, and so on, and at the same time to suggest a freshwater shrimp or sow bug. Basically it is meant to look like a proverbial grocery store to the quarry—which it does. The important element here is where these flies fish, rather than what they are supposed to represent. Bugs of this shape are bottom dwelling. They hide from predators among stones, weeds, and so on, and the predators know this, so this is the best clue to how and what to fish. I would add that if you are not losing flies, you are fishing this either incorrectly or in the wrong places. Be bold!

Moving steadily upstream and searching every "lie" is the hallmark of a good Czech Nymph.

Heaviest fly can go here to hold the midwater column

Keep the flies 18 in (0.5 m) apart or as required

TACKLE

See Jiri's Jig on page 87. It is exactly the same; in fact, you can use either in conjunction with the other.

VARIATIONS

A range of colors and sizes should be seen as essential. Have fun with it and experiment!

RED SPOT SHRIMP

NEIL PATTERSON, ADAPTED BY CHARLES JARDINE

Season: *All*
Type of fish: *Trout and grayling*

Neil Patterson introduced this fly to me. I think it is one of his greatest creations, although I have come to realize that any fly that comes from the jaws of a Patterson vise is worth adding to the fly box. (I should have put more of his flies in this book.) This pattern has, down the years, done amazing service for me—and not just on rivers. It is, was, and will, I suspect, remain at the forefront of my fly box, to call upon whenever I need a pattern for stalking and targeting large rainbows on small, clear stillwaters.

DIFFICULTY 5/10

MAKING THE FLY

1 With the hook in the vise, tie in the rib followed by the shell back. (If you want a tail, tie it in after the rib, but before the shell back.)

2 Make a neat underbody with all the materials smoothly bound to the shank. I can't begin to tell you how important this is. Any lumps or bumps at this stage will ruin the overall effect.

3 Add a layer of lead wire in exactly the same way as you did with the Czech Nymph, covering it with a layer of instant glue.

4 Dub the body in an even manner—again, as in the Czech Nymph.

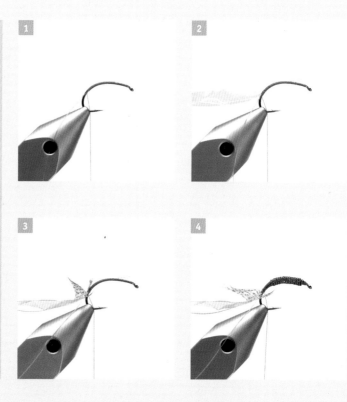

The essence of this fly is in the design and the way the weight is compacted, allowing it to both sink fast and look realistic, yet fish hookpoint uppermost so as not to get continually caught up. If you then add the target point, you will come to see this pattern as a favorite, too. I also now use it in conjunction with other somewhat similar patterns, namely Czech Nymphs, when grayling fishing in either the Czech or Polish style. It is a great journeyman, too. Rarely do I strongly encourage people to carry one certain pattern, but this is one of those occasions. Then again, I guess I could make a similar case for the other 49 flies in the book. Isn't that why I'm writing this book in the first place? Tie it, store it, use it.

Hook: Curved grub 10–14 weighted with turns of lead wire and shaped in the same way as in the Czech pattern (*see page 88*)

Thread: Olive 8/0

Tail (optional): Natural or olive-dyed English partridge

Rib: Copper or gold wire or clear nylon mono in 4 lb (1.8 kg)

Back: Clear building-grade PVC (the original) or Scud Back

Body: Mixed natural fur: seal's fur (sub) or hare's mask in a tan or olive color scheme

Spot: Fluorescent red or arc-chrome orange floss or wool

MATERIALS

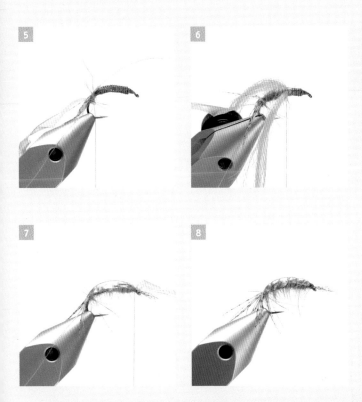

5 Halfway down, stop wrapping the dubbing and loop in a strand of fluorescent floss or wool. Secure this to either flank of the fly in this central area.

6 Continue with the dubbing toward the hook eye. You still have some work to do in this area, so leave space. Trim the floss/wool flush on either side of the fly.

7 Advance the shell back over the back and secure with the wraps of ribbing. In the original, the fly was ribbed prior to this, but I find the segmentation is better—and more durable—if you rib last.

8 The finished fly, complete with tails and breathers.

TACTICS

The Shrimp's design makes it perfect for conquering confused currents and cutting through the layers to reach trout lurking in holes between banks of weeds or in pockets. On stillwater the scenario is similar, except for the absence of flow: you spot your prize, watch to see what depth it is cruising, and—once you have made the calculation of the weight of the Shrimp and the time it will take to descend—launch the fly sufficiently far ahead of the quarry. Trout tend to take this fly just as it drops through their cruise path. If you have to retrieve it, then the Shrimp doesn't seem to work as well. It's the same with rivers: let the current do the work—your job is knowing when it has reached its destination and if the quarry has fallen for the trap.

My friend Mauro Mazzo with a fantastic early-season brown trout taken on a Shrimp.

The almost "mercurylike" bubble envelops the fly like the natural

The hackles look like chaotic legs

BEHAVIOR

Years ago we all thought the red spot denoted an egg cluster within the carapace. Then we learned it was actually a parasite. Either way, the trout don't seem to mind that much. There are few waters in the world, especially with a degree of alkalinity, where these crustaceans don't exist. And if they are there in numbers, the trout will not only feed avariciously on them, but put on weight like you wouldn't believe. I am glad to say a Czech Nymph version of the scud works very nicely indeed. The natural lives in and around subsurface vegetation and has an amazing capacity for speed, and when flitting about tends to swim sideways (many people have thought shrimp moved upside down, but, no, they do the side crawl). They are also most useful when they are more extended, rather than resting in the fetal position.

The natural in abundance! Spring creek scuds taken from a Pennsylvania river.

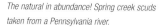

TACKLE
The usual suspects, really. For river fishing, an 8 ft 6 in (2.6 m) #4 or #5 rod, floating line, and, because of the fly's weight factor and the need for accuracy, I would keep the leader length down to about 9 ft or 10 ft (2.7–3 m). On stillwater, I'd use a #6 line and err toward a 12 ft (3.6 m) leader.

VARIATIONS
I tend to vary the body colors to accommodate gray species, light tan, olive, and so on. Actually, a pink Shrimp works alarmingly well!

ADAM SIKORA

Season: All
Type of fish: Trout and grayling

POLISH WOVEN NYMPH

The Polish Woven Nymph is all about grabbing depth and doing so quickly. Nowadays there are all types of preformed, loaded, and variously weighted hook designs, but when these flies first came to our attention it was the construction and choice of materials that held the key to overcoming the speed of the water. Mackerel skin, eelskin, pig bladder, and so on have all been used in Polish design, and for those who are a little squeamish about fiddling around with slippery bits of animals, floss is the perfect solution.

DIFFICULTY 8/10

MAKING THE FLY

1 With the appropriate hook in the vise, make a base layer of the thread wraps.

2 To weight the pattern, if you want a rounded shape, just make the usual close touching turns along the hook shank; if you want a flatter, almost wobblelike aspect, place a strand of lead wire along the shank, secure, then place a further layer of lead wraps over.

3 Make the whole area smooth and tapered and, as a detail, try placing an underbody of pearl Mylar over these turns.

4 Take two strands of body material of equal length and contrasting color and tie these on either side of the hook shank, just on the bend. Secure and detach the thread from the hook. It will not work otherwise!

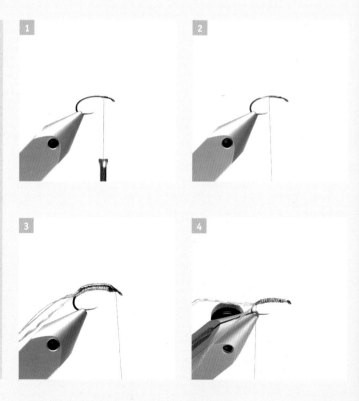

The concept revolves around defeating the water flow and plummeting the fly down through the layers, but I have noticed that it only works when it is constructed in the manner shown. I urge you to spend time with the initial construction of the design and get the weighting part just right, because it is this that will make the pattern twist and pirouette in the flow as it sinks, which is a large part of the attraction. It's primarily a river pattern and specifically for freestone waters—the rough-and-tumble, chuckling streams that are full of pockets, holes, riffles, and bouncy water. That said, I have actually done quite well with this pattern on stillwater, too, especially in the stalking/targeting role and when imitating lesser water boatman, *Corixa*. The actual weaving style suits the variegated back very well.

Hook: Curved grub 8–14. The one shown is a Czech barbless hook known as Kanepeck. Weight the hook with lead wraps exactly as shown in the pictures.

Thread: Black and cream or pale yellow 8/0

Rib (optional): Nylon mono 4 lb (1.8 kg)

Body: Underbody—optional turns over pearl Mylar followed by two strands of contrasting colored floss. Can be subtle, like cream and pale yellow, but usually brown and yellow, olive and yellow, etc.

Hackle: Small beard hackle of black or red brown cock hackle

Head: Ice Dub followed by ostrich herl

MATERIALS

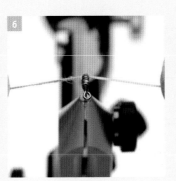

5 Turn the vise around so that the hook eye is facing you. Then, through an overhand knot with the two strands of body material, slip these over the eye so that the darkest color shows on top of the hook shank.

6 When tensioning the strands, apply equal pressure—this is vital for an even body, so it doesn't roll and get "skewwhiff." Just pull outward with equal pressure and form the ridges along the side as shown.

7 Repeat this procedure until you have covered at least three-quarters of the hook shank, then reattach the thread and form the thorax, having popped in a beard hackle if desired.

8 The completed fly with the thorax in place.

TACTICS

I tend to use a design like this in the middle position of a three-fly team and let it grab, hold, and stabilize this central area, fishing the lighter patterns above and below. It can be placed on the point, but it is the middle method that seems to work best for me. The style follows the broadly outlined Czech method: cast the team on a short line to an upstream position, allow the flies to dig in and descend, and, as they sink, follow them around with the rod tip at the same pace as the current. Maintaining control and line tension is crucial. The only real difference is that at the end of that maneuver you just hold: let the patterns swing and dance in this downstream position for a while—perhaps not on every cast, but at least the odd one during a run down a glide or riffle.

Lisa Isles, the past captain of the English Youth World Rivers team, studiously searches an ideal height and speed of water for the Polish Nymph, on the Teplá Vltava.

The weave looks like an insect's abdomen segments

By drawing on the line y can make the fly climb layers or fish dead-drift

The nymph as it descends

The shape allows it to cut through the water column rapidly

BEHAVIOR

Being another version of the Czech designs, it pretty much follows the same insect mimicry—caseless caddis (*Rhyacophila* and especially the *Hydropsyche* species). However, there are other areas that can be covered by this style of dressing, if not this specific pattern. I have mentioned *Corixa*, but the woven body suits almost any aquatic creature, because most have some degree of lighter abdominal section underneath. I have seen some stunning stonefly and damsel nymph designs incorporating this type of construction, but the pride of place must go to the sedge, either larva or pupa. Weaving just seems to add a very fishable dimension to the pattern.

The author's son Alex, and Midge his dog, get ready for a day's bugging—the dog usually catches the most!

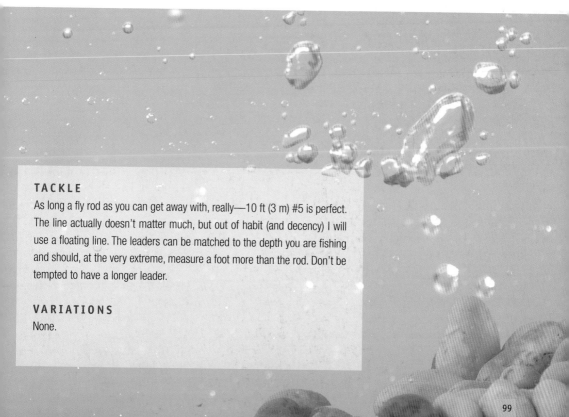

TACKLE

As long a fly rod as you can get away with, really—10 ft (3 m) #5 is perfect. The line actually doesn't matter much, but out of habit (and decency) I will use a floating line. The leaders can be matched to the depth you are fishing and should, at the very extreme, measure a foot more than the rod. Don't be tempted to have a longer leader.

VARIATIONS

None.

GORDON FRASER

Season: *Summer months*
Type of fish: *Trout and grayling*

FRASER'S SEDGE PUPA

Gordon Fraser is a man for whom I have huge respect; in his own way he has been instrumental in altering the attitudes of many British stillwater fishers and bringing them into the world of lean patterns and carefully observed, subtle details. The Fraser's Sedge Pupa embodies all the hallmarks of his careful reservoir wisdom, but it took a very close colleague, Paul Procter, to bring it to my attention in a river capacity.

DIFFICULTY 5/10

MAKING THE FLY

1 Tie in the ostrich herl strands so that they project over the hook eye and then, with the thread making touching turns down the shank, work in a strand of floss and take this down to, and just past, the hook bend.

2 Create a dubbing rope in the same way as the Czech Nymph style: not too tight nor segmented.

3 Wind the dubbing two-thirds of the way along the hook shank, followed by even turns of ribbing.

4 Cut a section of hen pheasant tail fibers close to the shaft, ensuring the tips are in alignment. You will need about eight to ten fibers, depending on the fly size: remember the tips will form the "legs" and be divided on both sides of the design, so there should be enough to accommodate this. Tie these in so that the tips face over the eye and have sufficient length, so that when

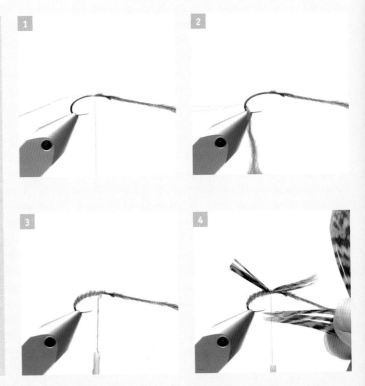

What I like about this pattern is that it uses materials that are both cheap and easy to get hold of. These materials are then used in an entirely innovative way, a bit like the Sawyer Pheasant Tail and Roman Moser's patterns. I particularly like the hallmark "hackling" procedure. But now the question: did Fraser get the idea from Al Troth, and did Al Troth get it from Polly Rosborough? And do the trout really care? Sometimes—and I hear and read this endlessly—people worry about where a pattern comes from. Be relaxed, tie it, fish it, and, importantly, just enjoy it for what it is!

Hook: Standard wet 10–14 (16)

Thread: 8/0 to harmonize with the body. I have found that the best color for general use is pale yellow/buff

Rib: Yellow floss

Body: Seal's fur (sub) in green, amber, yellow, cream, olive, gray, etc.

Thorax: Dubbed animal fur—hare's mask is ideal

Thorax pad: Hen pheasant tail

Hackle/legs: Hen pheasant tail tips folded back along the body

Head (optional): A turn or two of gray, black, or brown ostrich herl

MATERIALS

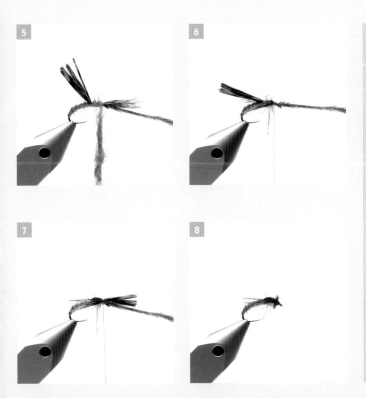

folded back along the thorax they reach at least halfway down the shank.

5 Dub and wind the thorax with the natural animal fur—an ordinary mono-directional dub using well-waxed thread is the one to use.

6 Leave room at the hook eye—this is important, because you still have some work to do.

7 Divide the hen pheasant tail tips into two equal sections. Fold these back along the body and secure with some thread wraps. Keep these to a minimum; you will then bring the main wing section over the thorax and secure at the hook eye.

8 Now wind and flourish the ostrich herl head: I have to admit it does add a little something to the design when wet.

TACTICS

A pattern like this can fulfill so many roles, from an additional pattern as a middle dropper when fishing in a "loch style," to a top dropper pattern when fishing in the Czech style on rivers. You can also use it on the point position of a team when fishing "spiders"— soft-hackles on smoother water. For the classic "sink and draw" technique, select a gold bead style of pattern—the Red Fox Squirrel Nymph is perfect. About 3–4 ft (0.9–1.2 m) above this weighty point fly you place the Fraser's Sedge Pupa. You cast out diagonally across the stream and let the current sweep them all around while you make a draw on the line. Stop, repeat, stop, and so on, until that cast is finished, then repeat. You can almost feel the fly lift, fall, and flutter with the pull and shudder of the current. Beware: takes can be brutal!

Tree cover, a shallow riffle—all perfect
situations to find caddis and use an imitation
during the daytime.

The air bubble in the dubbing mimics the natural aspect perfectly

The trailing fibers resemble the legs and wing case of the natural

BEHAVIOR

Caddis pupae, once free of larvahood, are active little beggars: the long paddlelike middle legs can actually allow them to swim quite strongly (there are some species that wander along the river bed, but we're not addressing those here) and they will make excursions to the surface, where they often drift inert for long periods—hence the style of fishing I have outlined. Of course, on stillwaters there isn't the flow to cause this activity but, seemingly, the caddis will still adopt the rise-and-fall zigzagging movement up to the surface. Let this be the clue to how the pattern is fished.

A grumpy brown trout about to be released, having fallen "foul" of a Sedge Pupa.

TACKLE
When fishing Sedge Pupae I would definitely opt for as long a fly rod as I can, given the circumstance, realistically get away with—9 ft (2.7 m) minimum, 10 ft (3 m) better, #4 or #5. Floating line, of course, but there are times when you might want to experiment with a wet-tip.

VARIATIONS
Change the body color dubbing to match the hatch in your area—sea green, amber, gray, tan, olive, etc.

EASY L.D.O. NYMPH

PAUL PROCTOR & CHARLES JARDINE

Season: All
Type of fish: Trout and grayling

Sooner or later, most fly tiers want to try their hand at tying something that actually looks like a creature that fish eat. Enter realistic fly tying. I, and so many others, have been seduced by Ollie Edwards' fly-dressing perspective on aquatic nature and the angling side of direct, calculated imitations. It tests us, and I honestly think we end up better fly dressers as a result.

DIFFICULTY 5/10

MAKING THE FLY

1 Prepare the hook by weighting it with turns of lead foil over a layer of thread. Make this smooth and then add the tails. Return the thread to the thoracic area and securely tie in a length of Spanflex.

2 Using very close turns of thread, secure the Spanflex at the bend and then wind in open turns as shown—only barely touching—up the hook shank.

3 Secure and add the thorax pad (Nymph Flexi-Body and feather fiber) so that they lie along the shank back. Now tie in a partridge hackle in the same way by the tip.

4 Dub the thorax with the soft fur.

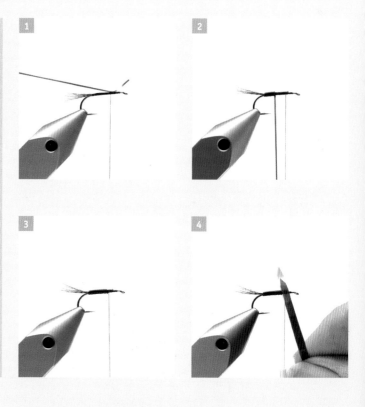

There is a problem though. In fact, there are several, with "close copies." In the first place, they take more time to tie and it's more aggravating when you lose them. Secondly, the nearer it is to the real creature, the more you have to know about the imitated insect's natural lifestyle to fish it well and effectively. This is not a bad thing, but there is far less margin for error. As I just mentioned, though, you end up being a better and more well-rounded fly fisher for it. This pattern is a halfway house, which I have to admit is more to my liking: fairly easy to construct, pretty close to the insect, but suggestive of other kindred forms.

Hook: 2X–3X long shank nymph hook loaded with turns of lead foil (adhesive lead strip that you cut and then wind: it is less bulky than lead wire)

Thread: Danville's Spiderweb

Tail: Olive-dyed partridge

Body: Nymph Flexi-Body or Spanflex

Thorax pad: As above with black pheasant tail fibers either side

Thorax: Olive-dyed pine squirrel or similar soft, variegated animal fur dubbing

Legs: Olive-dyed partridge

MATERIALS

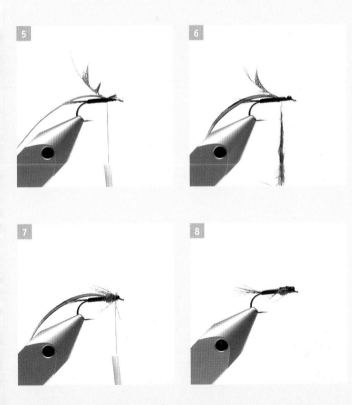

5 Add some preformed nylon eyes for added realism if required.

6 Bring the partridge feather forward and secure, ensuring the fibers stick out from the thorax in a semi or full, perpendicular configuration.

7 Make sure that you dub between the eyes.

8 Bring over the thorax cover and secure at the eye, then ease back between the eyes. Finish at this point as shown.

TACTICS

There are times when a Pheasant Tail or G.E. Nymph, amazingly, are shunned by the fish. That's when it's time to bring out this beauty. Just cast upstream to an observed quarry, assessing the depth of the trout (or grayling—they like these, too), and just watch the fish's movements for the "vital signs."

On rough-and-tumble waters—freestone types—placing the nymph on the point of a team of wet flies (spiders) gives you the perfect "anchor" to dig in the team and allow the flies above to dance to their deadly little river tune. Actually, when trout are rising to olives, more often than not it is the nymph that is taken, as opposed to the wet flies. No, I don't know why either!

John Goddard—the great man of fly fishing—casts using available care. His PVC nymph was the inspiration for patterns like this.

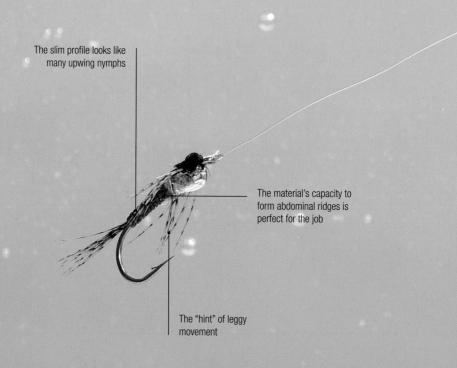

The slim profile looks like many upwing nymphs

The material's capacity to form abdominal ridges is perfect for the job

The "hint" of leggy movement

BEHAVIOR

This pattern is primarily an imitation of the large
dark olive *Baetis rhodani* (and of course the trout
know that!), but the basic design is suggestive of
a wider group than that. This whole category of
nymphs (the *Baetidae* are classified by anglers as
the agile darters), though differing hugely in color
and in size, mostly conform to an overall shape
that is sleek and agile. They use these attributes to
get themselves out of danger, or at least to attempt
to flee from hungry trout. This entire insect genus
is therefore of great interest to the fly fisher, and
on a global basis, because these types of flies can
be encountered throughout the world.

*Clear water, and a trout on "the fin"—perfect
for a design like the L.D.O.*

TACKLE
For classic upstream nymphing I would recommend you use a 9 ft (2.7 m)
rod and #4 floating line—even better if the fly line is a muted color: a green,
tan, or similar. Use a leader length of between 9 ft and 12 ft (2.7–3.6 m).
For wet fly/spider fishing, the same line will work, only with a 10 ft (3 m) rod
and a leader of nearer 14 ft (4.2 m); this will be perfect.

VARIATIONS
None, other than color and size.

RED FOX SQUIRREL NYMPH

DAVE WHITLOCK

Season: *All*
Type of fish: *Trout and grayling*

Dave Whitlock's design is revered the world over as a general representation of almost anything buggy, but sadly it just didn't seem to work for me. One day I was fishing with my buddy Paul Procter, who said I was missing a trick. The one element he had included in his versions was "leanness." This was absent from the original, and my versions were decidedly "tubby." I urge you to follow the slimmer route! They work a great deal better, in my opinion.

DIFFICULTY 5/10

MAKING THE FLY

1 Thread the bead on the hook, place in the vise, and add the thread. I use two threads: orange to start the pattern (to harmonize with the lighter dubbing), switching to the darker one when doing the thoracic area.

2 Run the thread to a point halfway down the shank and then tie in the tail. Try to get the tail tip in alignment. Add the rib at this point, too.

3 Plug the gap between the bead and the tail with some turns of lead wire. This will make the pattern much smoother and better tapered.

4 Blend the dubbing and then create a dubbing noodle, forming the taper. Start to make the body by winding the dubbing "rope" in touching turns.

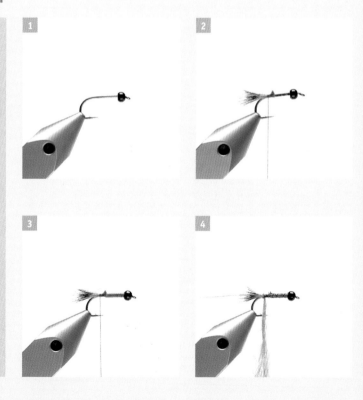

I am not going to say that this pattern has now gone into full take-off mode for me; it hasn't. But it's working far better now that I have slimmed it down—and the bead has also added an element of "catchability" to the design. Where I have found this pattern to have a distinct advantage is when I'm fishing for grayling on British waters in winter and need a general cased-caddis pattern on the point of my leader to act in the supporting role to the next pattern—one slightly smaller and lacking a real capacity for grabbing depth. The pattern's role on stillwaters should not be forgotten, either. I prefer the Hare's Ear in its many guises, but this is becoming a close second. Still, it's true what they say: if you don't use it, how are you going to catch with it?

Hook: 2X long nymph hook 8–16 loaded with lead wire and/or a bead (your choice): copper, gold, or colored

Thread: Black, chestnut brown, orange, or claret 8/0. For grayling fishing I use fluorescent red thread

Tail: Red fox squirrel guard hairs

Rib: Pearl Mylar or oval gold tinsel

Body: 50/50 blend of "orange" red fox squirrel belly fur and a similar colored Antron

Thorax cover: Pearl Mylar (optional)

Thorax: Charcoal Antron mixed 50/50 with red fox back fur

Hackle: Grouse or partridge in the smaller sizes

MATERIALS

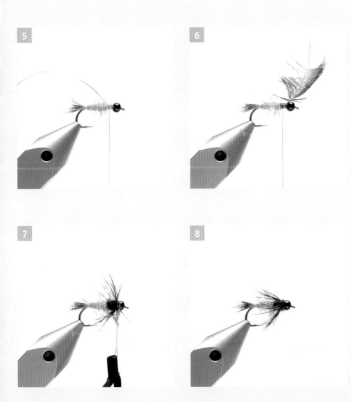

5 Cover two-thirds of the hook shank with the dubbing and then add (optional) the pearl Mylar thorax cover.

6 Change to the darker thread (optional) and then run the thread to just behind the bead and tie in, by the tip, a grouse or partridge hackle.

7 Form a small buglike thorax and wind the hackle for two turns.

8 Advance the Mylar thorax cover, tie it in between the turns of hackle and the bead, add some more dubbing to cover the working thread wraps, and whip finish.

Dwarfed by a western sky, two anglers fish the Henry's Fork just above Osborne Bridge in the fall. It's the perfect time to use small, lightweight nymphs like the Red Fox Squirrel to cover the plethora of species emerging at this time of year.

TACTICS

Place a Squirrel Nymph—incorporating the fluorescent red thread and usually a gold bead—on the point of the leader. If I'm adding further sections, I will use two 2 ft (0.6 m) sections in 5X. On the droppers I tend to place a smallish nymph (a 14–16 G.E. is perfect at the top), then a Czech Nymph in 10 or 12. Select water that is "riffly," but also holds deep pockets and pools. Cast upstream, let the flies sink and "grip" the water column, and then, when they have reached their maximum sink-point, stroke them gently through the layers in a smooth, arcing curve. It is speed fishing, but very effective.

Once again, the dubbing catches the fish-attracting "bubble"

The bead helps sink the pattern and adds to the thorax overall

BEHAVIOR

The problem here, like so many patterns in this book, is that the
Red Fox Squirrel Nymph is a general-purpose creation, designed to
meet a number of aquatic situations in a very nonspecific way.
My fly box is bulging with patterns like this—and I believe it's all
the better for it. I love presenting the trout (or grayling) with
options, suggesting that they—the quarry—should make up their
minds what the thing looks like, not me! I guess that this fly could
look like a scud, a hog louse, sow bug, cased caddis, caddis pupa—
a smorgasbord, actually. And that is where its effectiveness lies.
Having a pattern like this does not ask an amazing number of
questions of the angler. It's a case of just add water and fish the
thing (in the manner described), and enjoy the moment.

This Rhyacophila *larva is typical of the wide
range of aquatic forms that general nymphs like
the Red Fox can convey. There are, of course,
specific dressings for these key species, but it is
useful to have impressionistic patterns so that
the trout can decide what they represent.*

TACKLE

You will need a floating line (though you won't be using much of it), a 10 ft
(3 m) #5 fly rod, and a leader of about 12–14 ft (3.6–4.2 m) in total length.
The first 5 ft (1.5 m) is plaited or braided; at the base of this I have a tiny
silver stainless steel ring to which I attach my first strand of tippet, a 3 ft
(0.9 m) length of 5X. I then add a further tippet with a surgeon's knot,
holding a dropper length of about 4 in (10 cm). I always select the
downward-facing length of the dropper and trim off the upper length,
the piece projecting back to the rod. This is for strength and knot resilience.

VARIATIONS

I tie a number of designs with or without beads, and also vary the bead color
to meet the demands of various water types: dull for clear water and bright
beads for fast or colored water.

CHARLES JARDINE

Season: Throughout the fly-fishing year—nymphs are available to the quarry species almost every month, except for in extreme cold
Type of fish: Trout and grayling

G.E. NYMPH

This is my Pheasant Tail. It came about because, during my formative years on the chalk streams of Southern England, I found there were times when, for reasons best known to the trout, they just ignored Pheasant Tails and similar "Sawyer-esque" patterns. This was before the brave new world of Ollie Edwards and his remarkably lifelike designs that I enjoy fishing so much. However, even with something as cunning as the Large Dark Olive Nymph, or even the Easy L.D.O., there are elements of "stiffness"—a lack of life.

DIFFICULTY 4/10

MAKING THE FLY

1 With the hook in the vise, attach the thread and take it down the shank for a few turns. Then tie in the tailing fibers and rib.

2 Wrap the body with turns of lead foil—or not, if you want more of an emerger style.

3 Work in, right on the hook bend, about four to five feather fibers by their fine tips.

4 Wind these up the hook shank in open turns so that you get an even spread of feather fiber, and then rib in the same direction.

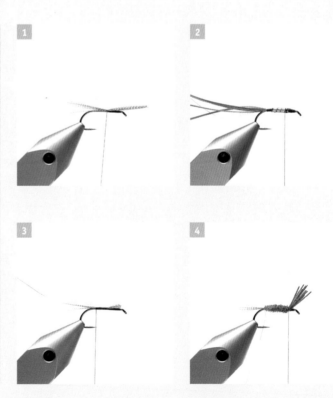

Natural fibers, and there is no doubt in my mind on this point, seem to be fueled by a zest for life that synthetics, no matter how superbly constructed and articulated, seem to lack. There is nothing extraordinary about this pattern, and it draws on a number of noted anglers of the time of Frank Sawyer, Richard Walker, and so on. It is just a fly based on what was in existence at the time and some pure bankside insect and trout observation—but I guess that's fly fishing. The test of any pattern is in its longevity; I still use the pattern (and that is some 20-odd years now), and the great thing is, the pattern has found a niche on stillwaters when the bigger olives—the lake and pond olives—start to emerge. All in all, it's a simple pattern that still has a role to play.

Hook: Standard wet 12–18 (14–16 being the most useful sizes). Weighted with lead foil sheet, or not, to suit. No beads, please.

Thread: Orange 8/0

Tail: 4–6 wood-duck fibers

Rib: Very fine silver wire

Body: Olive-dyed feather fiber (goose flank or swan—they used to be called cossett feathers)

Thorax cover: Dyed black feather fiber: pheasant tail, etc.

Thorax: Olive-dyed pine squirrel or similar soft animal dubbing

Hackle: Lemon wood duck tied either side of thorax

MATERIALS

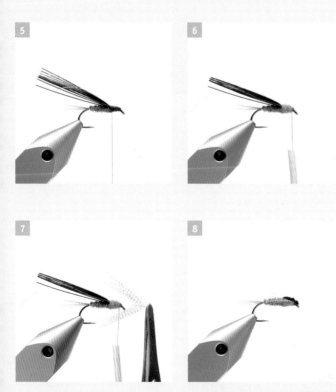

5 Trim the body material neatly away, and now add the black feather fibers to form the thorax cover.

6 Dub the thorax.

7 Now cut a "V" configuration in the wood duck flank feather as shown. Offer this up so that the "V" fits into the area immediately between the front of the thorax and the hook eye, and tie in so that the fibers sweep back.

8 Now advance the feather fiber thorax cover and tie it in. If you desire more detail, place a little dubbing by the hook eye, then double the feather fiber back and tie it in just behind the hook eye to form an almost eyelike effect. Finish at this point as shown.

TACTICS

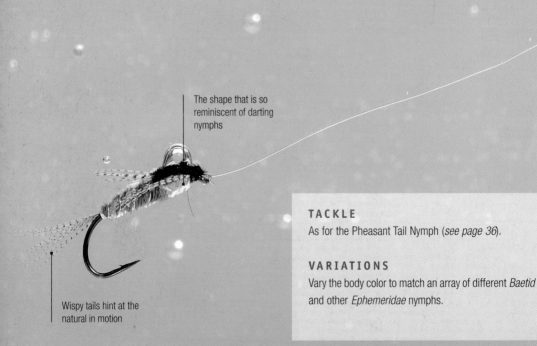

I have pretty much outlined all the various ways of fishing a pattern like this already. The one thing I would urge anyone to do, though, is observe the quarry closely. This might seem obvious, but I am utterly bemused to see how many anglers just cast and hope. The essential thing in dry fly fishing—and probably even more so in nymph fishing—is understanding the quarry's reaction to a natural fly and to your pattern when it is trying to emulate a natural. I urge you, therefore, to study both the fish and its world, and then to set about trying to catch it.

BEHAVIOR

So why is the thorax pad black? This is a peculiar color for a nymph—especially the smaller olives. It came about when I was looking at the nymphs in a confined space and it dawned on me that as they were about to hatch at the surface the thorax pad turned very dark, almost black. This seemed to be the case throughout, and was not confined to just one species. I think it must act as a trigger to the trout. There is nothing more stark in a light, watery environment than black. And this all came to me from a child's fishing net, a jar of water, and some small bugs. It's an interesting world.

The shape that is so reminiscent of darting nymphs

Wispy tails hint at the natural in motion

TACKLE
As for the Pheasant Tail Nymph (*see page 36*).

VARIATIONS
Vary the body color to match an array of different *Baetid* and other *Ephemeridae* nymphs.

THE CUTTING
EDGE ABOVE

ROMAN MOSER

Season: *Primarily high summer. Caddis can hatch from early spring through to late fall, but late spring and summer see the most hatches*
Type of fish: *Trout and grayling*

BALLOON CADDIS

Similar to how the Hopper did on stillwater, this pattern changed my angling life. A chance trip with the late Alan Bramley of Partridge Hook fame brought me into contact with one of the very finest river anglers I have seen, but also one of the world's truly innovative fly tiers: Roman Moser. Roman used his school-teaching background to turn the river into a type of schoolroom for anglers.

DIFFICULTY 5/10

MAKING THE FLY

1 Having secured the hook in the vise, cut a sliver of foam about one-eighth of an inch wide.

2 Now tie it in through the thorax on a bed of thread so that it protrudes over the hook eye. Make sure the turns of thread are touching, as you need to reduce the bulk of the foam.

3 Now run the thread back down the shank to the bend and work in a few fibers of a dubbing strand.

4 With the thread under tension, rotate the dubbing in a single direction around the core of thread. You will find that the tied-in fibers will cause the dubbing strand to twist and bind together. Advance the dubbing rope up the shank for about two-thirds of its length.

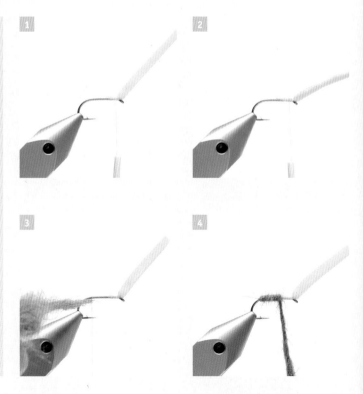

Roman is a phenomenal angler, caster, tactician—everything—but what elevates him to truly legendary status is the way he constructs flies. Like all great men, Roman conveys the complex simply. He can strip away all that is superfluous and get to the very heart of what he is trying to do and recreate. This takes skill and an awful lot of time in studying the creatures that he imitates, but it doesn't just stop there. Roman goes on to find the very material that conveys exactly what he needs from that specific pattern, and that can take him to some unusual places, believe me. Compared with most of his designs, this one is pretty normal and mainstream. We can only wonder at the mind behind it, and copy and fish the patterns. I know one thing: if Roman designed the fly, I will fish it.

Hook: 3X long shank wet fly 10–14

Thread: Pale yellow 8/0

Thorax pad: Buttercup yellow Ethafoam/Polycelon strip

Body: Irise Dub (if you can get it), Ice Dub, or similar blend in pale yellow, mid-yellow, tan, gray, olive etc. to imitate the caddis species predominating

Wing: Roe or dark yearling elk, or white tail deer hair fibers

Thorax (optional): Same as for the body, but two tones darker

MATERIALS

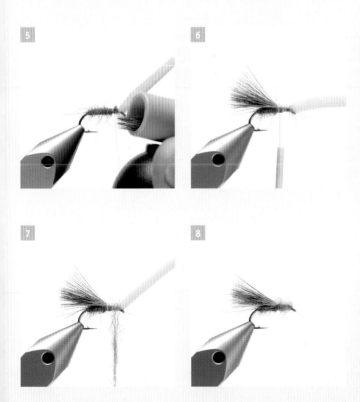

5 Prepare the deer hair—you will need about 20 individual fibers. Comb out the under-fur at the base of the fibers and tap the tips into alignment in a hair stacker.

6 Tie these in immediately after the dubbed abdomen.

7 Dub a small thorax if you think it will help your chances, or do what we all do and just make some turns of thread.

8 Bring the foam back over the eye and thorax, and secure immediately where you tied in the deer hair wing. Also make your whip finish at this point over the foam and trim the surplus foam. Be careful not to trim out the wing, too.

The noted Italian fly fisher and instructor Mauro Mazzo adjusts his leader and fly choice at sedge time on the Vaslesia river in North Italy.

TACTICS

This is one of Roman's searching patterns at the surface. It is as at home on stillwater as it is on smooth currents. The idea is to fish this just a little bit faster than the current to create a disturbance. There is no question in my mind that a disturbance in the surface zone attracts rather than deters our quarry. This is a fly that will do just that. However, it is on rivers that the Balloon Caddis is in its element. There I tend to select riffles and areas that have a certain *joi de vivre* about them and then let the river do most of the work during the retrieve; all I do is nudge it along the surface a little faster. I warn you: takes can be explosive.

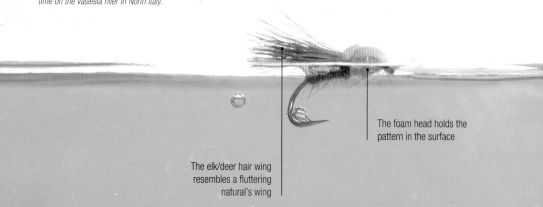

The foam head holds the pattern in the surface

The elk/deer hair wing resembles a fluttering natural's wing

BEHAVIOR

This is where the Moser genius truly shines through. His minute observation of fly life, and also the abundance of caddis on his home waters, suggested to him that the natural would run for quite some distance, just subsurface, even in rough water, propelled by its strong paddle-like leggy appendages, before hatching; hence the retrieve. Then the head area would burst open and out onto the surface would clamber the natural—the adult fly. From the surface it then either flies or makes a run for it along the top, to the bank. All this you can do with this design. Roman is also insistent that the trigger with caddis species is the yellow—exactly what it represents I have no idea, but it is present on just about all his designs. And if Moser puts it there, so do I.

A perfect backdrop and current for fishing caddis patterns. It is this type of water (the Austrian River Traun) that the Balloon Caddis was originally designed for and it is in such areas that the pattern can work both dead drift or "teased" across the current to make a disturbance.

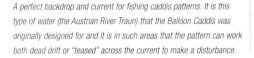

TACKLE
A 9 ft (2.7 m) rod taking a #5 line is perfect. Moser used to use a very fast rod indeed, and leaders and lines that he designed himself for this task; lately, I have been fishing this design and many others on my trusty 10 ft (3 m) #4 and I have to say that the extra length when articulating the design is a real joy and offers a tactical advantage when it comes to bringing the fly to life.

VARIATIONS
None, other than the body color—and if you brave the thorax, too.

KAJ KIRKEBY

Season: During adult caddis activity (summer and early fall months)
Type of fish: *Trout and grayling*

THE ENVELOPE SEDGE

You may be wondering why there is a need to have two adult caddis patterns and why anyone would go to such lengths to fashion a wing. I will explain. Because of the universal distribution of caddis species, there is a good chance that trout, if present, will eat them. This poses some problems. There is no denying the versatility or attraction provided by patterns like the Elk Hair Caddis, but it is a fast—or at least broken—water design. The makeup of it alludes to realism, rather than paints a picture of it. Enter this design.

DIFFICULTY 6/10

MAKING THE FLY

1 Make the wing by sandwiching it as shown in the self-adhesive envelope sleeve. Trim the encased feather to the size and shape required for the hatches in your area. It's great fun.

2 Tie in a CDC feather by the stalk at the hook eye once the layer of thread has been attached to the shank.

3 Run the thread to the hook bend and then dub a body of chopped CDC fibers up the shank for about two-thirds of its length.

4 Once at the thoracic area, stop and then wind the CDC hackle by the tip of the feather—this is to allude to the creature's legs and offer both flotation and a hint of scuttling movement.

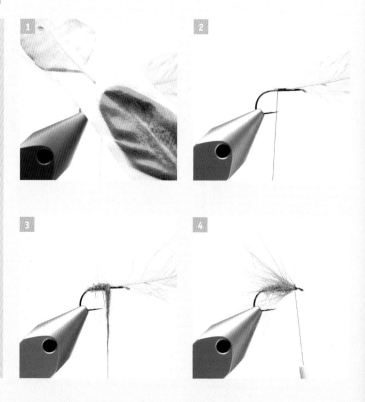

It is dedicated to flat water—areas where the river glides or the lake is tranquil. It has a softer, more gauzy outline, and offers the trout a semi-real profile and closer color scheme. It is just stunning on all counts. I first saw it being tied at the Danish FFF fly festival and my jaw dropped. It was so simple, so well-conceived, and just, well, fun to tie. The problem has been obtaining the right winging material support. I would love to be able to give you the exact envelope... but I am sure, though, that a judicious search will find one. This pattern just goes to prove the rather odd and unstinting lengths we will go to to baffle and befuddle a trout. Is it any wonder that rational people think fishers are odd?

Hook: Dry fly fine 10–20

Thread: To match color scheme of species and wing and body material in 8/0–12/0

Body: Dubbed chopped CDC or soft fur dubbing (muskrat, beaver, etc.)

Main wing: Grouse, English partridge, or similar game bird flank feather sandwiched or stuck to a self-adhesive clear postage envelope (clear tape can work, but not as well)

Secondary wing: A few Coq-de-Leon fibers to act as a support

Thorax/hackle: Spun and trimmed CDC fibers in a dubbing loop

MATERIALS

5 Add a secondary wing of Coq-de-Leon fibers or yearling elk. This will also act as a support and add a little bit of glister to moderate the somewhat stark nature of the wing.

6 Add the envelope wing folded over these fibers so that it extends slightly beyond the hook bend in a tentlike configuration. Place several individual CDC fibers in a dubbing loop (*see page 15*).

7 Wind the dubbed CDC head as shown to form a soft, fluffy thorax akin to the natural.

8 Very carefully, with a dubbing needle, pick some of the fibers out from the spun area to act as a fluffy support at the head area.

*The joy of dry fly and catch and release.
A Pennsylvania brown trout lives to fight
another day.*

TACTICS

 I have already suggested that this is a pattern for the quieter flows. That doesn't mean it shouldn't be fished in an animated way, but this pattern does suit a more dead-drift style of fishing. When you find an area that is either in the grip of caddis activity and looks like a holding area for trout, or where you can actually see trout actively feeding, your job is to cast a little upstream and let the fly come down the current under its own steam. As the evening draws on, you might think about trying a little "animation."

The CDC gives
a feeling of light,
buoyant life

The head of the
fly "at rest" having
been skated

BEHAVIOR

Oddly, I have found that when fishing the Sedge—especially when the naturals are active—there seems to be a very distinct pattern to how you address the behavior and the fishing. When you see the caddis either hatching or active during full daylight, a moving imitation seems to offer little attraction unless the water is broken. However, once the light starts to drain from the sky, twitching the fly—either by the use of your rod tip or by hand stripping movements—seems to be the way to go. Whether this is because as the light fades the fish increasingly hunt by vibration, or whether they home in on the movement of the fly, I don't know. Don't overdo this movement, though, especially on smooth water, or you will drown your fly.

The Large Cinnamon Sedge (here), Potomophylax latipennis, *is reminiscent of many caddis species. A "detailed" pattern like the Envelope, by varying the wing coloration and the actual fly size, can also convey many different species and will appeal to fastidious fish feeding in calmer areas.*

TACKLE

Usual dry fly gear is the way to go here and use that long rod (10 ft [3 m] #4)! It will assist both the presentation and the ability to skate and skitter the fly. Use a long leader and a tippet to match the fly size. Be warned: takes can be savage, but there is also a need for delicacy; let that guide your tippet choice.

VARIATIONS

By using different feathers in the "Envelope" and altering the body color, a host of different species can be imitated. Best thing would be to try to note the key hatches, obtain a sample, then imitate size, color, and shape.

RENE HARROP

Season: Mayflies can hatch at any time throughout the year, but are most active from early spring through to late fall
Type of fish: Trout and grayling

TRANSITION DUN

Rene Harrop has long been a beacon for dry fly precision. He embodies the same economic genius as Roman Moser, but in an entirely different way. The Harrop world is brilliantly observed, but he has other methods for recreating what he sees. Mind you, the water he fishes—Henry's Fork—has forced a very different set of complex angling circumstances upon him. He has made this river his life study, and the patterns that have sprung from his countless hours of watching will, I promise, work anywhere in the world.

DIFFICULTY 5/10

MAKING THE FLY

1 With the hook in the vise, run the thread in touching turns down the shank to the bend and place a tiny ball of dubbing there.

2 Tie in just behind the dubbing ball four Coq-de-Leon fibers so that they flare out like little outriggers.

3 Now tie in the biot quill. Experiment to determine which side you want showing. One will have a filigree of tiny hairlike barbules, and the other will be smooth. It's your choice.

4 Wind the quill now, gripped by the hackle pliers. These will give you fantastic accuracy and a delicate touch and make an otherwise tiresome job with your fingers comparatively easy.

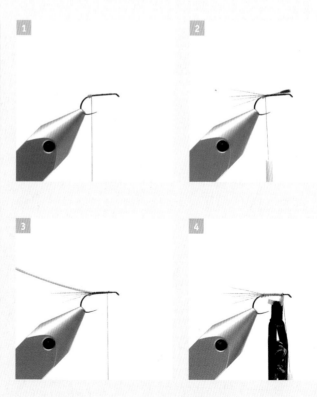

To be fair, most of his patterns tend to be imitations of mayflies of one type or another, and over recent years, like so many others, he has fallen for the magic material—CDC. OK, this fluff from the base of a duck's back is not a universal panacea, but in Harrop's hand and in his vise, it's pretty darn close. Also, it is far more durable than the precise and sublime designs that he and his wife once crafted with mallard quill and other less robust materials. The idea behind this and other designs of his is to recreate the diaphanous and complex stages of the mayfly's emergence, then to defeat the truly intricate currents and the fastidious tastes of tailwater trout at their most finicky. In this he has succeeded, and if you take the time and pains to tie these designs you probably will, too.

Hook: Light wire dry fly 14–24

Thread: 8/0–12/0 pale yellow, tan, gray, olive, etc.

Tail: Coq-de-Leon fibers

Body: Soft animal fur in olive and tan shades to match your natural (beaver or muskrat under-fur is perfect as the dubbing ball) followed by a turkey biot in a harmonizing color (olive, tan, etc.)

Wing: CDC fibers (two complete feathers)

Thorax: As for body, but a tone or two darker

MATERIALS

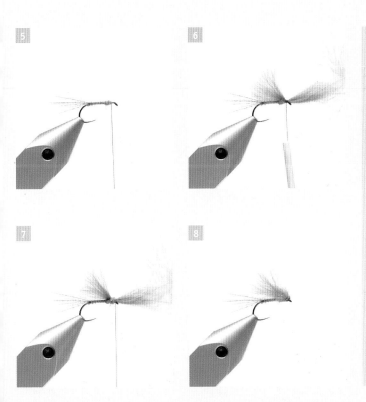

5 Dub a tiny thorax of the soft fur—a bit like an extended area of the dubbing ball at the bend, and just as tight and precise.

6 Tie in two CDC feathers and anchor them against this dubbed thorax.

7 Place some more dubbing over the thread wraps. You have to be very precise here and, while I do not usually use wax on patterns like this, here I would suggest it may be advantageous.

8 Now comes the finishing touch. The bottom of the feathers (the stubby part) can be brought back on either side of the body, secured, and then either a bit more dubbing or merely thread wraps can be added to finish. Then trim these side panels to the desired length.

TACTICS

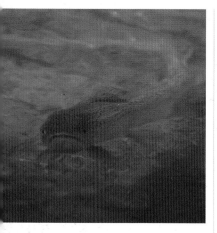

As I have already mentioned, this is a smooth-water fly. It is designed to meet the fussy demands of trout that seemingly view their world through a magnifying glass, so it is all about observation of the area you are likely to fish. I find it extraordinary that fishers often decide the entire day's game plan before they have even gotten out of the car or strung a rod. Get on the water, and only then make your decisions. You have to, when fishing any water, size it up. Look for the rising fish, signs of activity, recent hatches—a spider web on a bridge or bankside bush is perfect for providing clues to recent hatches. The size and color of the insect will then determine what fly to put on, and what size of tippet. The flat water calls loudly for long, fine tippets and long leaders fished on light lines.

Shall I? Shan't I? The Transition Dun was designed for moments like this!

The tippet partially sunk

The fly caught in the surface film

The "outrigger" tails provide stability

BEHAVIOR

The water, and not necessarily the actual fly, tends to determine the behavior. Smooth water, by its nature, is going to have created a comparatively thick surface film; for many insects, this is a huge (sometimes fatal) barrier to try to overcome. Enter the trout—grinning. As practiced hunters, trout will not pass up any easy dinner. Fortunately for the angler, rather than leading to difficulty and ultraselectivity, this can be an Achilles heel of sorts. When mayflies hatch, some tend to get stuck fast, some are crippled, some even die in the process, and most will be eaten in this prone, floating state before making the transition to adulthood. Enter this pattern: a low-riding killer.

The grandeur of nature. The last-chance section of Henry's Fork.

TACKLE

I like my 10 ft (3 m) #4 for this style—but then I would! Usually one would match the rod to the river, and in the case of rivers the size of Henry's Fork, a 9 ft (2.7 m) rod is perfect when matched to a #4 line. Keep leaders tapered and long, combined with a gossamerlike tippet—see 5X–7X as your norm. (Oh, and wade and approach carefully and gently. This style of fishing is as much about you and how you present your flies as it is about the fly itself!)

VARIATIONS

The design stays the same, but the body color varies to match the hatch.

LIVELY MAYFLY

Had it not been for American fly fisher and tier Chauncy Lively's wonderful book *Chauncy Lively's Flybox*, many of today's patterns would not exist—it was that influential. As I was still feeling my way through the complex menagerie of fly fishing and tying, this book shone as a beacon of what could be achieved with just a modicum of ability, common sense, and some fly-tying knowledge. I merely adapted this pattern to suit the needs of British waters and that wonderful crescendo of activity—the mayfly hatch.

CHARLES JARDINE

Season: Mid to late spring and early summer, when various large mayfly species hatch, but also, if tied in an appropriate size, whenever you have a hatch of medium-to-large mayflies

Type of fish: *Trout (and salmon!)*

DIFFICULTY 8/10

MAKING THE FLY

1 With the hook in the vise, bring together at least 20 lemon-yellow wood duck flank feathers and manipulate them so that they are tip to tip and neat. Offer these up and tie them in so they face forward over the eye (advanced). Ensure the length is sufficient so that when raised upright they extend at least halfway down the deer hair body.

2 Tie in the pheasant tail fibers to reach back at least three times the hook length.

3 Align a bunch of elk or deer hair fibers (15 or so is fine). Tie these in just along the shank from the hook bend.

4 Bring the fibers together around the tailing material by holding the tip and just circling the bobbin. Use continuous movements, spiraling up the deer hair body and making a succession of securing wraps at the

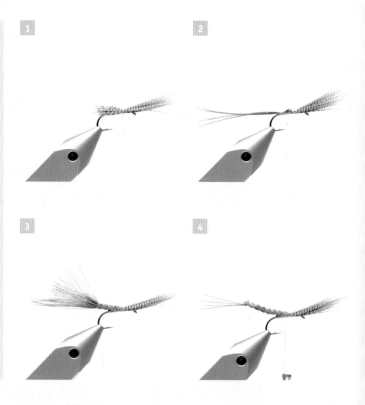

This is an extraordinary period that has been called the "Mayfly Carnival," among other things. For me, it truly is a celebration, a point that seems to bring nature together in jubilation. The time of year is lovely, the rivers are looking their finest, the trout are in great shape, small birds and animals have fledged and are enjoying their first summer, and then there is this fly—a natural bounty for many. Bring in the trout! The fact that the mayfly is so important—and big—has obviously meant that it has gripped the attentions of fly dressers for generations. It is a fly that just begs to be imitated, and this is my stab at it.

Hook: Medium gauge dry fly hook 10–12

Thread: Tan or pale yellow 12/0

Tail: 4 cock pheasant tail fibers

Body: A cluster of deer or elk hair fibers

Rib: The same thread as above

Wing: Carolina lemon wood duck fibers or mandarin duck flank fibers

Thorax: Tan, mixed with orange soft animal fur dubbing (or Fly Rite Poly)

Hackle: Grizzly cock hackle optionally mixed with natural red

MATERIALS

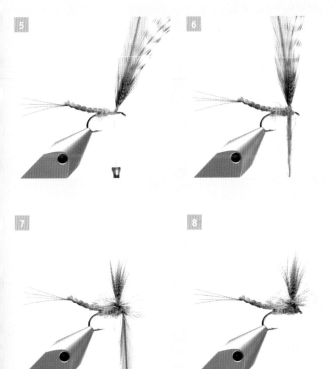

end (one-and-a-half to two times the length of the hook shank), then returning the thread back down the body, mirroring the turns to craft an evenly ridged, buoyant, extended body.

5 Tie in two hackles—big flies need a fair amount of support. Create a post of thread around the wing fibers, attaching the two hackles as you go.

6 Now dub the body over the clipped deer hair strands and take this up to just short of the wing.

7 Finish by winding the hackle in the usual parachute style, starting at the top and working your way down the post.

8 Hopefully you should end up with something like this!

The Gingerbeer Stretch on the hallowed waters of Hampshire's River Test in the U.K. was the birthplace of this fly. Also depicted is a very young Charles Jardine, actually catching and landing a trout.

TACTICS

Make sure that the leader you use has sufficient taper to actually turn this bulky fly over: an ill-tapered leader can ruin your presentation completely. The problem lies in the fly's bulk and the drag of this amount of material being pitched through the air, so you need to be certain that the tippet is robust enough to turn over the fly and ensure that your pattern does not look like a piece of fuzz on a bedspring. The tippet must be stiff enough to convey the package to the target but still embody the element of deception. Beyond those issues, it just boils down to good old presentation.

The high wing: visible to the angler, a trigger to the trout

The detached body displaying its natural imitative attributes

The parachute hackle ensures the fly stays "in" the film

BEHAVIOR

The dun or drake is the second phase of the mayfly's lifecycle, the point at which the fly has burst through its nymphal incarcerations, pushed through the surface and rested on it, then taken to the air to mate. The angler will see all of this enacted a hundred—maybe a thousand—times during a heavy hatch of mayfly. Early in the two-week slot, when this insect is at its majestic height of hatching, trout will really feast on it, but toward the end the trout can become very picky indeed.

A natural adult mayfly in all her glory. The males die soon after the frenzy of the mating swarm. The females wait for low light before laying their eggs and falling dying to the water's surface.

This brings us to a phenomenon known as sequential feeding, a state in which the trout will tend to take, say, every second, third, or fourth natural coming over its position, but not every one. To stand any chance, you have to monitor the situation and make sure your fly fits into the sequence—fun, but it can be uniquely frustrating.

TACKLE

My choice here would be a 9 ft (2.7 m) rod and a #5 line—perfect for turning flies over in the wind, or just purely managing the bulk of the pattern. I have mentioned leaders; I would err from the 5X to the 4X and maybe even higher breaking strain. And a floating line, of course.

VARIATIONS

None.

PJ DUN

I wouldn't blame you in the slightest here for being just a little confused. I have just mentioned The Mayfly and now I am mentioning A Mayfly—and there is a difference. The first one is the name that U.K. fly fishers bestow on two insects, both *Ephemeridae*—*danica* and *vulgata*—and the second mayfly is the generic term that all scientists (and U.S. fly fishers) use to describe up-wing flies that in England might also be called olives. It can get a bit confusing.

MARC PETITJEAN

Season: Whenever there's a small mayfly hatch

Type of fish: All game fish and some coarse fish

DIFFICULTY 7/10

MAKING THE FLY

1 With the hook in the vise and the thread attached, take your CDC twiddling stick, or merely gather some long-fibered CDC barbules together with your fingers, and tie them into the thoracic area in a bunch.

2 Now loop a section of floss or a very thin sliver of foam around the thread, slide this into the position shown, and secure. Doubling the material in this way causes minimum buildup.

3 Catch in the tails with thread wraps, take the thread to the hook bend, and then noodle dub in a soft animal fur body (you can use chopped CDC too). Construct a neat dubbed body.

4 Run this dubbing to a point just short of the wing in the thoracic area.

While I think it would be inaccurate to suggest that Marc Petitjean was the first to devise flies from CDC, it would be correct to suggest he has done more than most to popularize this material—great for us, but not good for trout globally! One of the difficulties that I and others have had is understanding that a fly so unkempt can outwit such a sophisticated and preoccupied feeding fish in the way that it does; and how such little material can actually float a fly. Much has been made of the flotation properties of CDC, the natural waterproofing oils, etc., and there's no doubt the softness of the natural material and the way it behaves has turned many of us into myopic CDC dry fly fishers. Nonetheless, I would insist that there is still a case for hackle—as you will see.

Hook: Light wire dry fly 12–20

Thread: 8/0–12/0

Tail: Coq-de-Leon fibers

Body: Soft animal fur—beaver or muskrat under-fur in drab olive, pale yellow, or tan to match your intended species. Fly Rite Poly works well, too.

Wing: CDC fibers grabbed in a bundle

Thorax cover: Floss or foam to harmonize with the body

Thorax: As for the body but maybe a tone or two darker

MATERIALS

5 Pull the floss back between the CDC clumps that have been divided equally.

6 Invert the hook in the vise so that you can bring a layer of dubbing in on the underside and create that all-too-important thoracic bump so prevalent in the natural fly.

7 Secure the floss immediately behind the wing (on the hook bend side). If you use a contrasting material such as fluorescent floss you can get a visual "sighter" that will enhance your fishing and your observation of the pattern.

8 If you want a neater pattern, you can trim the tips of the wing into a more "acceptable" winglike vision. I am not sure whether the trout actually care one way or another!

A Paradise Valley (MT) spring creek; home of fussy trout and the need for patterns like the PJ Dun.

TACTICS

I could just say, "Get a suitable tippet, find a rising trout, cast this out, land the trout, release the trout and...be happy." I honestly have that much faith in this pattern. Let me give you an example. One evening, when fishing a tiny river populated by super wary little wild brown trout, I decided to experiment. I put on the biggest PJ Dun I could find—a size 12. Given that the naturals would be best represented on a size 18 or 20, it looked gargantuan and ludicrous. Anyway, I cast out near a rising fish and the fish, and others (although thankfully not all), just tilted, edged nearer the surface, sidled up to this preposterous looking thing on the surface, and sipped it in—utterly confidently. Use this fly!

A very lifelike wing, when seen from below

Outrigger tail for support

The contrasting thorax, so often a "trigger" for the trout

BEHAVIOR

The PJ Dun represents the fly just as it is about to
hatch off the water. In fact, if you alter the color
scheme—well, the body—to a claret or orange CDC,
you can accurately imitate the final stage, too,
known as the spinner or imago, the spent female
fly lying inert in the water after the exhaustion
of laying her precious cargo of eggs. Amazingly,
the same design will work, but just wearing a
slightly different set of clothes. So, in essence,
with this pattern you have a fly that can cover two
dramatically different and important parts of the lifecycle.
I would get close to the natural's size a little more than I alluded to
in the experiment, though. If you just look on the water and identify
the stage of a fly's life that looks vulnerable, you probably won't go
too far wrong.

*A glorious brown trout is carefully cradled
before being released, having fallen for a
PJ Dun.*

TACKLE
I would just go with the usual dry fly river gear that you are familiar with,
erring more toward the lighter lines than the heavier—#3, #4, or #5. I have,
though, been experimenting with braided/plaited leaders for fishing this
design incorporating a fairly long tippet, and they are working well.

VARIATIONS
None, except for the CDC wing color perhaps, or a body color change.

DAVE WHITLOCK

Season: High summer/early fall
Type of fish: Trout

WHIT'S HOPPER

The number of hopper patterns nowadays is utterly bewildering. Some have rubber legs that look like a bundle of elastic bands; others have eyes, presumably to see where they are going; and most float so high and ride the current in such a way that they look as if you could use them as life jackets. And then there is the Whit's Hopper. This design and the parachute Schroder design are the ones that I use, and I think most guides in the Western U.S. would do the same.

DIFFICULTY 9/10

MAKING THE FLY

1 Run the thread in touching turns along the shank (leaving a bare area by the hook eye to effect easy deer hair spinning), tying in the tailing material and the stripped cock hackle stalk as you go.

2 At the hook bend, tie in the wool by the end, throw a loop as shown, and then secure this in such way that you can then run the longer wool strand in touching turns to form a non-tapering smooth body along three-quarters of the hook shank.

3 Now palmer the hackle (select a hackle with a short fiber length, certainly no longer that the hook gape) along the body in an open spiral and secure where the body ends.

4 Prepare and tap into alignment 15–20 elk hair fibers. Tie these in as you would for the Elk Hair Caddis. Prepare and offer up the trimmed feather fiber wing.

The reason is simple; they float deeper in the water, which may seem like an odd statement, but stay with it! When you design a fly, it's a matter of more than just manipulating material around a hook in a reasonably coherent way. You have to know how the fly will behave in or on the water, and how that appearance translates to the fish. Knowing how your pattern will behave, or what ambitions you have for it, will be determined by the choice of material. That is why I love this pattern—it is so wonderfully well-observed. OK, more modern materials are available, but for me the deer hair gives the fly the texture of the natural in a crunchy sort of way. Crucially, deer hair also ensures that the pattern sits low in the film, like the natural and unlike foam, and I honestly believe it is a far better catcher of trout.

Hook: Long shank 6–10

Thread: Black or dark brown 6/0

Tail: Yellow wool in a loop and red/orange cock hackle fibers (8–14)

Hackle: Natural red cock hackle

Body: Yellow wool

Wing 1: Elk hair

Wing 2: Oak turkey sprayed with vinyl artist's fixative and then clipped to shape

Legs: Knotted, clipped (very short/stubby fiber barbules) cock hackle stalk

Head: Whitetail or mule deer combed, tapped into alignment, and then spun

MATERIALS

5 Fold the feather fiber wing over the elk hair. Secure with wraps of thread.

6 Form and prepare the legs by trimming the fibers close to the stalk. Knot these, then offer them up on both sides of the wing. Secure and trim both the legs and the wings.

7 Prepare, comb, tap, then offer up a cluster of deer hair fibers. The number depends on the hook size, but the initial batch should have about 40 to 50. With tips facing the hook point, make a loose revolution of thread around the center of the hair. Spread the fibers evenly around the shank. Make another turn of thread. Gradually increase the thread pressure, causing the hair to flare. Once flared to the maximum, continue to wind through the hair until it stops spinning. Repeat with a second cluster of deer hair.

8 Make four straight cuts with serrated scissors, then trim to the shape desired.

Elk feeding in Yellowstone National Park: home of the fly—and the material (probably!).

TACTICS

Essentially, I fish this pattern upstream and usually in conjunction with a small nymph (a 16 Troth Pheasant Tail or G.E. Nymph) or another dry fly (a small Caddis or the like) tied on a tippet coming off the hook bend. I fish fast. This is a "cast, drift the fly, pick off, move, cast again" type of fishing—short lining, rather than long, and really the dry fly equivalent of Czech nymphing. I always imagine that a big fly will evoke a huge water upheaval like a whale breaching, but when trout rise to hoppers they do so, I think, in the knowledge that they are large, worth the effort, and unlikely to get away, so they take their time and just sip them in.

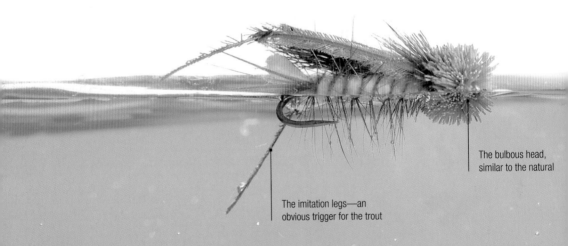

The bulbous head, similar to the natural

The imitation legs—an obvious trigger for the trout

BEHAVIOR

Grasshoppers seem to thrive in warm weather. They are energized by the heat, and if the wind gets up in the afternoon then there is danger of the grasshopper ending up swimming. Lucky trout! This suggests when and where to fish the pattern—from mid-morning onward, and near bushes and tall grasses. More generally, bankside zones on rivers like the Madison, Yellowstone, the South Fork of the Snake—even Henry's Fork—tend to have good concentrations of fish. They are there for the food and the cover that make the bank zone a prime lie, and these rivers are not unique in this respect.

Why we imitate the natural: the hopper in all its natural chirping glory!

TACKLE

Because of the conditions I have mentioned, and the fact that this is a big, air-resistant fly to hurl about, a fast-actioned 9 ft (2.7 m) #5 or #6 fly rod and matching floating line are ideal. I would try to keep the leader as long as possible, but that will probably be 10 ft (3 m) at most. A 4X tippet is good. A fine tippet only allows the fly to hinge, making casting terrible and turnover worse.

VARIATIONS

None. If a lower-riding pattern for smoother flows is required, then try a Schroder's Hopper.

ANTZ

CHARLES JARDINE

Season: Summer
Type of fish: Trout and grayling

I never thought that I would ever, ever, have believed that an ant would be a vital part of my fly box. The very idea! Yet, as I type, there in the corner of my fishing room are my fly boxes, and in them are ants. Brown ones, big ones, little ones, some with wings, some chewed, but all in all I carry a lot. Why? Because they work, that's why.

DIFFICULTY 5/10

MAKING THE FLY

1 Over a layer of black thread, select two goose biots or strands of feather fiber and tie these in, so that the blunt (non-tapered) end protrudes over the hook eye.

2 In the same area, now tie in a strand of black foam.

3 Trim out the thicker end of the feather fiber, run the thread to the hook bend, and attach the dubbing in the noodle style.

4 Take this dubbing to a point halfway up the hook shank. Then bring the foam back over this dubbed area and secure this, too, in this middle section.

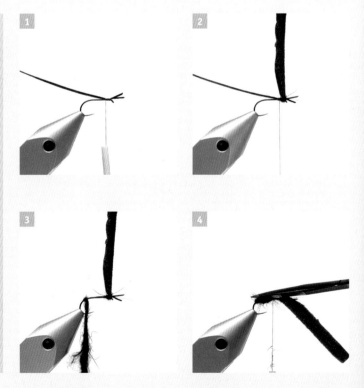

Years ago, I was inspired—energized—by a book called *In the Ring of the Rise* by Pennsylvanian trout fishing genius Vince Marinaro. It changed my mind and influenced a great many things in my fishing life; but especially my use of terrestrials. To a Brit this was relatively uncharted territory. OK, we had a few patterns, and there was some vague impression of an ant somewhere in the lineup. We also knew the value of a pattern like this on doldrum days in mid-summer on stillwater when the winged adults can tumble waterward and trigger a feeding frenzy, but these were sideshows to the more refined (so we thought) mainstream fishing, especially dry fly fishing. How wrong can you be! Now, through the enlightenment of many American authors and subsequent fly patterns, we have seen the light.

Hook: 14–20 (16 being arguably the most useful)
Thread: Black 12/0
Antennae: Feather fiber strand x 2
First shell back: Strip of black foam
First body: Black muskrat dubbing
Legs: Fibers of black/peacock Crystal Hair
Second shell back: Black foam strip
Second body: Black muskrat dubbing

MATERIALS

5 Loop in two or three strands of Crystal Hair and secure, with figure-eight turns of thread so that they protrude from either side of the body.

6 For the second half of the body, basically repeat step 4, but in reverse.

7 I strive to finish in the middle as opposed the head area, because this enhances the "waist" effect that is such a feature of the natural creature. If you want to craft an adult version, it is easy to add a pair of wings in the thoracic region, but I tend to just hint at the wings by tying in a bit of white polypropylene when I put in the legs.

8 This is the Chernobyl Ant, so beloved on western rivers like the Snake where it is used more as an attractor than a real ant. You can purchase the strip, then all you do is attach the foam "fore and aft" and add the legs in these areas. So simple.

Tom Baltz, the noted Pennsylvanian fly fisher, is a firm advocate of terrestrials on his native streams. Here, Tom cradles a Yellow Breeches brown trout that sipped in a terrestrial under a canopy of trees.

TACTICS

Because of the nature of the natural creature, feeding on terrestrials can happen almost anywhere and on almost any water, although it is mainly a summer phenomenon. Gentle wading (if fishing rivers), light lines, and long leaders are required. The great thing about ants is the fact they can be the key that unlocks the proverbial door when nothing is stirring on the water. Suddenly, seemingly from nowhere, comes that gentle sip and gulp of a fish feeding, but on what? The chances are, ants are to blame. Bear in mind that a trout taking flies opportunistically in this way will tend to drift back down to the lower layers, so fish the pattern just a little above where the last rise was. We call this "leading" the trout—casting sufficiently far above the fish's position for it to have a chance to see the fly and react.

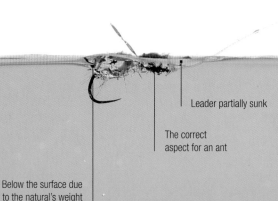

Leader partially sunk

The correct aspect for an ant

Below the surface due to the natural's weight

BEHAVIOR

I really don't want you to form the impression that this is solely a river situation. I have known times on lakes when the ant has been crucial to doing business and closing the deal on catching trout. I can vividly recall a blisteringly hot, energy-sapping late August day when the water surface was suddenly thick with adult flying ants that had mistimed their flight onto dry land. I don't know how the trout knew, but some sense grabbed them and thrust them up from the cooler layers many feet below, and they were just going nuts. Had we not had an ant pattern to tie onto the leader, that opportunity would have just floated by. More usually, though, you would fish your fly near grassy overhangs, under overhanging trees, and so on.

Henry's Fork: another river that can be "unlocked" by the use of an ant. In many very difficult complex hatch periods and in "technical" fishing, the ant can be a real code and hatch breaker.

TACKLE

Any of the usual lightweight dry fly stuff is great for this pattern—I would definitely err toward the long and light on this one, though; perhaps a 10 ft (3 m) #4 rod.

VARIATIONS

None really, although you can take foam to almost any floating situation, as the Chernobyl Ant demonstrates!

FOAM FLASH BEETLE

CHARLES JARDINE & OTHERS

Season: Summer months
Type of fish: Trout and other surface-feeding species

With any book like this there is necessarily going to be duplication. The information about the ant (*see page 140*) could just as easily apply to the beetle featured here—fly tying and fishing are like that. But there *are* some intrinsic differences. The Foam Flash Beetle—in fact, any beetle pattern—is probably more diverse and frequently used than the ant. A beetle can be a recurring theme that crops up on different water types over a very protracted period of the season, and at almost any time of the year.

DIFFICULTY 6/10

MAKING THE FLY

1 Work in the antennae over a layer of thread in the thoracic area as you did with the Antz. You can trim these to size at this stage.

2 Run the thread to a point halfway down the shank, catch in one single hen hackle flat on the shank as shown, and secure at the bend. Try to ensure that it is concave side down.

3 Now add the foam back, followed by the Medallion wing sheet, both at the hook bend.

4 Take the thread to a point about half to three-quarters of the way up the hook shank to secure the back, return to the bend, and noodle dub the Ice Dub along the body.

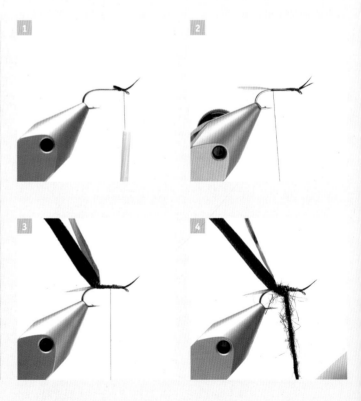

There are times when fishing on a reservoir, in seemingly hopeless conditions, you can get a fish to take a beetle pattern. All you need is the occasional erratic rise, just enough to suggest that the odd fish is "looking up," and away you go: cast out and, well...keep alert. It is much the same on rivers. A recent trip to the spring creeks in Pennsylvania emphasized this point. Even if the fish were fixating on tiny Tricos (or worse, not feeding at all), once you had identified a trout's position you could pop out a beetle with some firm hope that more often than not you would get at least some response—and usually a favorable one. So, alongside my burgeoning collection of ants is another of beetles, which in fact gets dipped into slightly more often.

Hook: Dry fly, wide gape, 12–20
Thread: Black 12/0
Antennae: Black feather fiber
"Tail": Pale blue dun hen hackle
Back 1: Strip of black foam
Back 2: Peacock colored plastic sheet (Medallion)
Body: Black/peacock Ice Dub
Legs: Black rubber or black/peacock Crystal Hair

MATERIALS

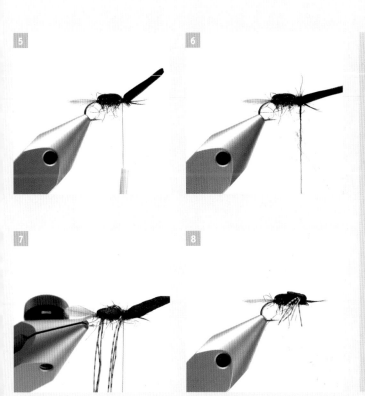

5 On reaching the half to three-quarter mark on the shank, stop dubbing, bring over the Medallion sheet followed by the foam, and secure. Do not trim.

6 Make a "waist" with a small amount of dubbing and add on either side some rubber legs as shown, or use Crystal Hair. I prefer the rubber legs.

7 Run the thread over the shell back to the hook eye, add some more dubbing, and return this back to the area where the legs have been tied in.

8 Fold and return the shell back to this area. Secure and finish with a minimum amount of whip-finish turns. Note: You need both the fore and aft areas to be bulbous and almost spilling over the edge of the hook.

TACTICS

 When fishing on stillwater, I will watch the wind lanes like a hawk. This is where the beetles will be blown and congregate—and so will the trout. On rivers I concentrate my efforts in and around trees, or anywhere that might suggest a beetle-like home. Don't worry about banging this design in! The natural is a bulky old character, and when it collides with water it makes an impact! Trout will be expecting a less-than-delicate landing. In fact, when a fly like this hits the water with a resounding "plop," it can trigger a reaction. Fly fishing is not for the faint-hearted!

BEHAVIOR

While I have covered this in other areas, it is worth noting that beetles come in all shapes (well, some are longer and some are thinner), sizes, and colors. Remember to make some in brown colors, too. You might be wondering about the tail. I first saw this crafted by A.K. Best, the infamous fly tier and foil for John Geirach. He noted that when crash-diving on water, the natural invariably had one wing poking out from the hard carapace. He thought he'd add this. I thought I would, too. It certainly hasn't done any harm!

Similar to the ant, the fly must be "in" the surface film

The legs will create an illusion of life

TACKLE
The same as for the Antz—the usual dry fly gear.

VARIATIONS
None, but you could supplant the use of foam with that of dyed (black, brown, etc.) deer hair brought over the back in a shellback configuration and, in so doing, have a lower-riding pattern still.

MY WORLD IN A BOX:
10 RIVER FAVORITES

OLIVER EDWARDS

Season: All
Type of fish: Game and other
predatory species

SCULPIN

Sculpin patterns are legion, but to some U.K. anglers they're comparatively unknown. There are two very good reasons for this. First, people have been known to be in fear of their lives for using anything even slightly larger than a caddis on many U.K. rivers. Secondly, the British know the fish as a bullhead or miller's thumb—not a sculpin. They are the same thing, though. This pattern is a design from that astonishing Englishman Ollie Edwards, crafted after fishing with Dave Whitlock on his U.K. home waters of the Wharfe.

DIFFICULTY 8/10

MAKING THE FLY

1 With the hook in the vise (make sure it is firmly attached) place the weight in the center of the shank and build up a smooth taper on either side with turns of thread. At the hook bend tie in the rib and start a dubbing noodle.

2 Dub the body. Then, from a well-tanned rabbit pelt, using a sharp blade or scalpel, cut a slim, pointed coffin shape. Cut on the skin side only, not the fur side. This way you will cause minimal disruption to the actual fur.

3 At the finely cut tip, place a dab of instant glue on the skin and fold the tip of the fur strip under, sticking skin to skin and forming an almost Mohawk-like hair piece. This will be the tail when trimmed. Let this cure.

4 Tie in the rabbit strip at the point shown and rib through the strip in the Matuka style (*see page 21*).

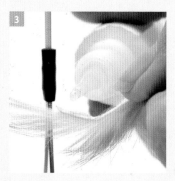

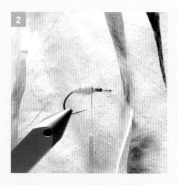

This is a refinement of the simple patterns familiar to U.S. fly fishers. These patterns have, over the last 20 years or so, edged from the impressionistic Muddlers through the more calculated designs that have become synonymous with fishing for big brown trout in the fall—especially in the west—and now embrace patterns such as Double Bunnies and other streamers. It is a form of fishing that is great fun; to hurl something like this into maelstrom currents, in and around boulders and fallen obstacles, seeking the cantankerous older brown trout, is to experience real adrenaline-fueled fly fishing. Try it wherever you are, but please just make sure of the rules governing the fishery before doing so!

Hook: A saltwater 6–2 loaded with turns of lead wire

Thread: Dynema

Tail: None

Rib: 4 lb (1.8 kg) nylon or oval gold tinsel

Body: Cream-colored soft animal fur or dubbing

Gills: Red dubbing

Pectorals: Grouse flank feather or English partridge

Wing: Cream/tan shaped rabbit Zonker strip

Head: Spun sheep's wool (known as sculpin wool) anointed with an adhesive eye on either side

MATERIALS

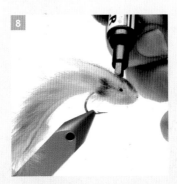

5 Place a turn of red dubbing in front of the Zonker strip then, on either side of the wing, place a fur or feather hackle for the Sculpin's pectoral fins.

6 Take a chunk of sheep's wool, place this on the underside of the hook, and secure it with several firm wraps of thread. Do the same again with a slightly darker color on the upper side of the hook. With finger and thumb pressure, pull both sections of wool back against themselves and secure the turns at the head. There should be an equal amount of wool all around the shank. Trim this to the shape in the image with sharp serrated scissors.

7 Glue a small plastic eye (these can be bought pre-formed from a specialist outlet) on each side.

8 Tone the head with a waterproof marker to create the right coloration for the species/variations where you fish.

A flat creek in Wyoming. A deep meadow stream that can respond to a carefully fished Sculpin in the holes.

TACTICS

Either use a full sunk line in order to reach the areas where few flies venture, or (my favorite) use a floating line but with a suitable density of tip looped into the floating line (mostly very fast-sinking/type 7). Then locate the areas. Look for anything like a lair. Big trout, especially brown trout, love sanctuary and the "harder to get at" the better. By casting amid these places you will certainly lose flies and leaders, but the prize outweighs the pain. If you see a boulder, just try "high sticking," almost Czech nymphing, a Sculpin in front and behind. In other areas, cast the pattern a little upstream, let the current grip the fly as it sinks, then tweak it a little faster than the flow in a sweeping downstream movement over the river bed. The takes can be savage!

The build up of head is a vital part of this pattern

The mobility of this fly ensures its success

BEHAVIOR

Having now made the case for a pattern like this, another can be made for other creatures: crayfish (crawdads), stickleback, minnows, shiners, and so on. The fact is, if it is nutritious and moves in a seductive way, then trout tend to see it as food. Trout of all species are among the most aggressive of feeders—a point that might be hard to address when they are only quietly and selectively sipping down Tricos and Caenis, but that is the reality. In a river system there are a great many edible creatures like this—probably far more than you think—that hug the bottom going about their little lives, and trout certainly know it! The stones are the clue as to where to fish the imitation. Your job is to get that fly down there and then move it in a way that the natural would behave: darts, flits, and short panicky little moves.

A rainbow trout lurks in an undercut bank flanked by boulders, just waiting for baitfish to cross its path. Stones, rocks, and coves offer trout a prime lie and the perfect habitat for sculpins. The imitation Sculpin is also designed with enough weight to reach such lairs.

The eyes are an important "trigger" to the trout

TACKLE
You will need tough tippets: 8–12 lb (3.6–5.4 kg) is usual in order to turn the pattern over. I suggest using a steeply tapered leader and then adding a shorter tippet section.

VARIATIONS
- Craig Matthew's Woolhead Sculpin
- Dave Whitlock's "original" Sculpin
- Muddler Minnow
- Double Bunny/Zonker

ENGLAND YOUTH FLY-FISHING TEAM

Season: All

Type of fish: Trout, grayling, and coarse fish

VLAD THE IMPALER

I have found that sleep deprivation has a wonderful way of consolidating a fly pattern. I had to tie this pattern for three solid evenings and very early mornings to fuel the rapacious needs of the England Youth World team when they were fishing in the Czech Republic. This particular design is a variation of the one that was being used to deadly effect by their Czech guide, Vit. This is an adaptation for a wider variety of water, substituting the all-peacock body for the slimmer profile you see here.

DIFFICULTY 4/10

MAKING THE FLY

1 Slip a bead on the hook. I prefer the drilled and slotted kind; they seem to be more forgiving of a wider range of hook sizes and shapes. I also prefer the faceted Disco Beads.

2 Secure the bead in the conventional way with turns of thread, but if you are using the "slot" style, an interesting angle can be constructed that will ensure the hook point rides uppermost by jamming the bead in the position shown with successive thread wraps.

3 Now secure the area by the bead, and then tie in a short-fibered, fairly soft cock hackle.

4 Add the strands of red floss (four to six strands should do it) at this stage, and also the rib.

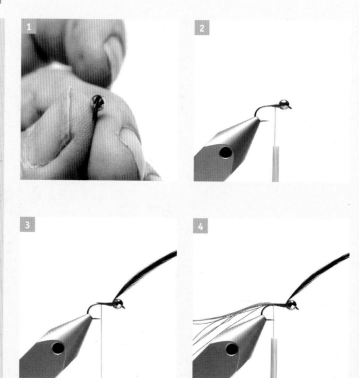

It could be argued, of course, that it is nothing more than a Red Tag. No dispute there. But this pattern has been a revelation since it forced its way into our collective fly box several years ago. In fact, I would argue that over time it has been one of the most consistent designs for both trout and grayling when fishing faster freestone flows. It is truly effective. The other great thing about this design is that it knows no geographic barriers, and just seems to be at home wherever it is fished.

Hook: Kanepeck 10–16 or TMC 103 BL 11–17

Thread: Red 8/0

Hackle: Natural red cock hackle (Indian is softer) short in the fiber

Tail: Red fluorescent wool or floss

Rib: Fine gold (or copper) wire

Body: Cock pheasant tail fibers

Thorax: Peacock Ice Dub (or a single strand of peacock herl) followed by pink after the hackle is wound

MATERIALS

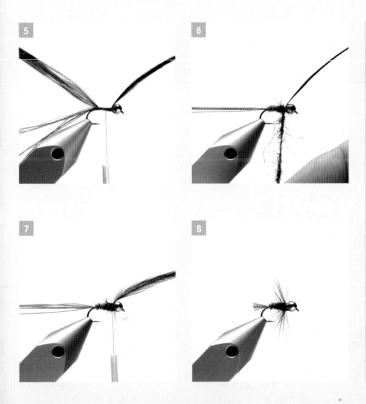

5 At the bend, tie in the cock pheasant tail fibers. I would advise about six to eight individual fibers for a size 12. I would also suggest that you trim and even up the tips, ensuring you tie these in with a minimal amount of thread wraps so that you don't get unevenness along the shank.

6 Wind the body in touching turns, but flat, not in a "rope" style. Rib in the conventional way. Secure, and then add a small amount of peacock Ice Dub or a strand of peacock herl to form a contrasting thorax.

7 Build a shoulder of red floss tying thread then wind the head hackle over this.

8 Add a small section of dubbing between the bead and the hackle. Pink is preferred by both trout and grayling. Then trim the tail.

A perfect "run" on the River Wye in the U.K. for the Impaler.

TACTICS

This fly is great for any situation, but one style that particularly suits it is the "rolling" or "stroked" nymph. This is a multiple fly tactic, but consists of a Vlad on the point. The weight of the bead is determined by the force of the current, so it is a good idea to carry a range, with ordinary brass beads on some and tungsten on others. Above you can have a couple of Mary-Rambos, a Czech Nymph, Pheasant Tail, or whatever. The leader with tippet and dropper attached is then cast upstream, no more than two rod lengths, and allowed to dig in and sink to its maximum extent. It is then brought through the water column by use of the line hand and the rod tip in a sweeping, tensioned, arcing curve. It is utterly deadly and a great way to search a wide variety of water types.

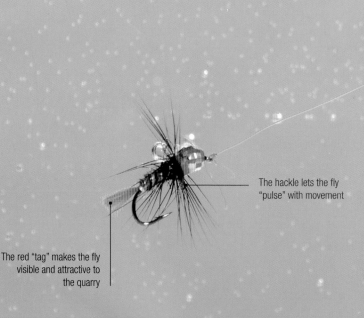

The hackle lets the fly "pulse" with movement

The red "tag" makes the fly visible and attractive to the quarry

BEHAVIOR

Because this pattern looks like nothing on Earth and is all about how it is fished rather than what it resembles, I would urge that you absorb the Tactics information and then try it on a stream near you as soon as possible. Having said that, the combination of bright red, red-brown, and peacock is such a recurring theme through fly-fishing history, it must mean something to the fish; goodness knows what exactly. I suppose it could be a vague notional caddis—although that seems a little far-fetched. Mind you, in the flows and the way that this pattern is fished, trout have such little time to assess the flies' authenticity that the color scheme might just trigger a reaction. We are back to finding that talking trout again—or at least a cooperative and articulate grayling.

Grayling love this pattern—anything with a touch of red seems to trigger a reaction, as this prime fish taken from Wiltshire's River Avon at Nether Avon in the U.K. would testify; spurning a Pheasant Tail on the home water in favor of the Impaler.

TACKLE

A 10 ft (3 m) #5 fly rod is ideal for this style, although you might want to use a shorter rod if fishing smaller rivers. Just reduce everything accordingly. A fairly robust length of leader (16–18 ft [4.8–5.4 m]) with the first part being a steeply tapered section ending in a small ring to attach the tippet and dropper lengths from the fly line is also key to the method; this will enable the flies to turn over with a minimum amount of line out of the rod tip—certainly not the critical first 30-odd feet (9-odd meters)! Braided or furled leaders are a real advantage in this role.

VARIATIONS

None, but you could change the tail color and the color of the bead. If the water is very clear and the quarry "spooky," try a dark bead or a silver one.

CHARLES JARDINE

Season: *All*
Type of fish: *Trout and grayling*

C.J. BUG

Wild places hold a mesmerizing attraction for anglers, and especially fly fishers. We crave desolate backdrops and wild trout, but things change when you live in such places. What were once playgrounds become places that offer variation on a grand scale, and each season beckons with both joy and exploration. That was what it was like when I lived halfway up a mountain in Wales: the rivers were wild there, as were the grayling and trout that eked out their lives in those extremities.

DIFFICULTY 5/10

MAKING THE FLY

1 Thread the hook with a suitable bead and then wind a layer of touching thread turns along the shank.

2 Tie in the CDC at the bead area and then work in the rib, followed by the pearl Mylar. Ensure that the Mylar is situated on top of the shank and maintains this position throughout the initial stages.

3 Carry the thread all the way around the hook bend and begin the dubbing rope in the now "approved" and familiar fashion.

4 Dub the body up to the thoracic area and then bring the Mylar back over the fly. The back tends to want to slide one way or another, but try to situate it exactly in the center.

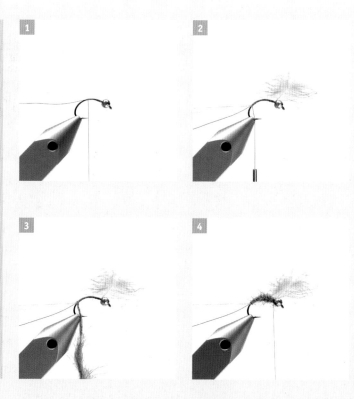

That almost day-to-day contact allowed me to indulge and decipher patterns and techniques; it was a period of mining a rich natural lode of knowledge and new discoveries. This is a pattern that came about from that time. I wanted a general-purpose design that echoed the world in which it was being fished, reached the areas where the quarry lived, then gave those fish a general representation of the creatures that they ate. It worked there and became the backbone of my adventures in the untamed landscape. Happily, it has worked on many other rivers, too, but as soon as I tether it to the tippet—no matter where I am—my mind tumbles back to slate riverbeds and impossibly clear water, the plaintive mew of distant buzzards, and the call of sheep. Funny what a fly can evoke.

Hook: Curved grub (light wire) 10–16 threaded with a brass or tungsten bead
Thread: Red 8/0
Hackle: Natural CDC feather
Tail: None
Rib: Copper wire (fine/small)
Back: Medium pearl Mylar
Body: Hare's mask well mixed with some strands of orange and amber fur or Antron (90% natural:10% color)
Thorax: Red thread and a small collar of peacock Ice Dub

MATERIALS

5 This job will be made a great deal easier when you start winding the wire rib. Keep the turns even and fairly open. Aim to place five or six turns along the shank. Make sure your winding pressure does not take the Mylar to the far side of the hook.

6 Trim, and now merely wind the CDC; it will look fluffy and funny and ungainly, but don't worry. It's what it looks like in the water that counts.

7 Form a small thorax in front of the hackle with the thread wraps, followed by a small amount—maybe two or three turns—of dubbed Ice Dub.

8 The finished fly should look like this—a little!

A lovely winter grayling, about to be slipped back into an English chalk stream—the Wiltshire Avon. In years gone by these beautiful fish were seen as vermin and culled. Now, they are rightly seen as an esteemed quarry and an important part of the river structure.

TACTICS

The 'Bug can be fished in any way you like, but two very different tactics suit it well. The first is the upstream deep nymph, for fishing—when allowed—on spring creeks: U.S. and European anglers will probably find it extraordinary that nymph fishing is still outlawed on many U.K. waters. Be that as it may, this is the pattern I use on these flows when I want to conquer deeper areas, hatch pools, and slots between weed beds. The idea is to cast far enough upstream for the fly to reach the quarry's holding area and then let it drift (dead-drift), seemingly unattached, toward the intended victim. The second is to use the 'Bug as a point fly when needing something of a lighter tone than the Vlad, but in similar weights and capacity. Just roll it through the layers, under a tensioned line, in an arcing sweep to the surface.

CDC has extraordinary properties subsurface

The "bubble" looks like an ascending pupa

The "disco"/faceted bead ensures attraction through light

BEHAVIOR

Once again, this fly is based on a whole raft of
different insects and not just one specifically.
If I look in my fly box there are, honestly, very
few that I would call direct imitations of the
natural world. Instead, I paint my subsurface
canvas with a very wide impressionistic brush
stroke. This fly is designed to resemble caddis,
scuds, sow bugs, or just about anything else
tan, beige, gray, buggy, and reasonably crunchy.
Beyond that? Well, trout and grayling like their
food available, and this is what this pattern is supposed to be:
general and impressionistic...and available...on their level.

An angler fishes the upper River Wye in Wales
in the U.K. during the late fall. It was on this
river that the fly was conceived, for both trout
and grayling (it has also caught the odd Atlantic
salmon). Now, the pattern's boundaries are
global, consistently taking fish the world over.

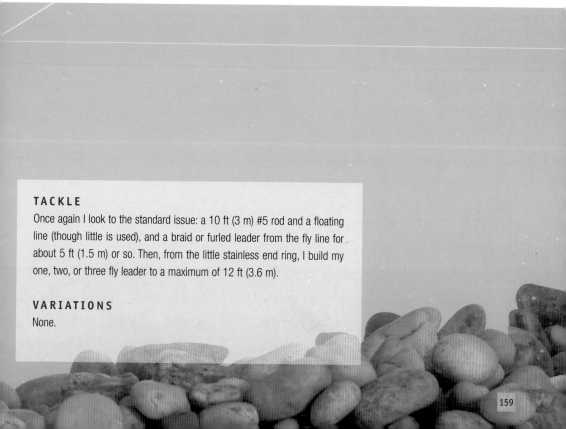

TACKLE

Once again I look to the standard issue: a 10 ft (3 m) #5 rod and a floating
line (though little is used), and a braid or furled leader from the fly line for
about 5 ft (1.5 m) or so. Then, from the little stainless end ring, I build my
one, two, or three fly leader to a maximum of 12 ft (3.6 m).

VARIATIONS
None.

THE MARY-RAMBO

SIMON ROBINSON
&
ANDREW RAMSDEN

Season: All
Type of fish: *Trout and grayling*

Of all the comparatively recent nymph designs, this little beauty has developed into one of the most consistent fish-takers in a whole gamut of different conditions. It is the development of two key members of the English fly-fishing squad: the late Andrew Ramsden, who died so suddenly and dreadfully early in life, and Simon Robinson, the renowned Northern England fly fisher who has won plaudits for his fly rod approach throughout trout-fishing circles. It takes great anglers to conceive simple patterns. This is a great pattern.

DIFFICULTY 4/10

MAKING THE FLY

1 Thread the bead on the hook; the TMC 103 BL is the hook of choice.

2 Attach the thread at the thorax area just behind the bead, and almost immediately tie in the tail.

3 Run the thread to the hook bend and tie in the body material. If you are using quill, tie this at the wider, more segmented end with minimum turns; if you are using pheasant tail fibers, tie these in by the fine tips. If you are using the thread as the body just run another layer up the shank.

4 If you are using pheasant tail or quill, place a layer of instant glue along the thread wraps for extra support and substance.

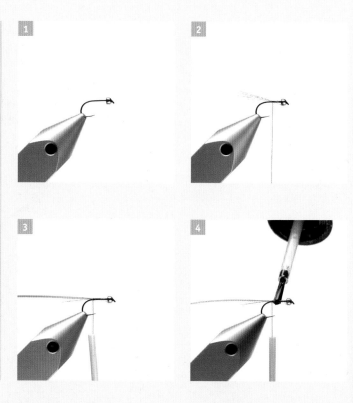

The secret lies in its slim profile. Trout seem to take flies far more readily when the pattern is in a state of undress. I have lost count of the number of waters this fly has conquered—and usually after the local anglers have denigrated something so small and vague as being a waste of time. This fly does tend to have the last laugh. I think that the case with this pattern is similar in many ways to that of wet flies/spiders, in that they do not set alarm bells ringing in the thoughts (if they have these, which I seriously doubt) of the quarry; there is no threat. As someone once said: "Trout—any fish—haven't got hands. The only way that they can determine whether it is any good to eat or not is to either run and hide or put in their mouths." Enter the angler.

Hook: TMC 103 BL 13–21

Thread: Micro/ 8/0 to match the body—olive, claret, black

Tail: 3–6 Coq-de-Leon fibers

Body: Stripped peacock quill (natural or dyed), pheasant tail fibers, or thread

Thorax cover: Pearl Mylar (small for tiny sizes, medium for the larger)

Thorax: Peacock Ice Dub

MATERIALS

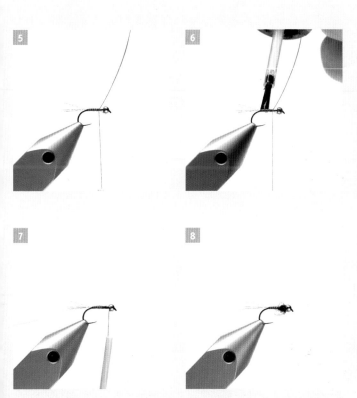

5 Run the body material up the shank in touching turns. Keep the whole thing very slim indeed.

6 If you have used a quill body, I suggest that you whip finish after crafting the body, then place a further layer of instant glue over the turns and set aside to dry for an hour or two.

7 Reattach the thread and add a thorax cover of pearl Mylar.

8 Dub the thorax with the peacock Ice Dub, bring the pearl Mylar over, and you are done.

Simon Robinson, one of the co-originators, and river guru John Tyzak, affectionately known as "J.T.," select a winning team.

TACTICS

Of course, you can use this nymph in any capacity you care to, but it excels when used in conjunction with a floating—and to some extent sacrificial—dry fly, such as the Beast-Hammer (a variation on a Klinkhammer, having a foam post as opposed to the usual polypropylene, to enhance buoyancy). Used in this way, it (or "they" if you are using two!) is the foundation stone of that deadly style of quick-fire fishing known as duo or trio. It is hard to think of a more effective or useful style than this in the modern era of fly fishing. Its ability to search water quickly and methodically is unsurpassed, in my opinion. (*For details of this technique, please see page 68.*)

The slim shape conveys much in the insect kingdom

BEHAVIOR

On the face of it, these flies look nothing like the real thing, but looks can be deceptive. I placed one next to a cluster of similarly colored mayfly nymphs—the agile, darting, large, dark olive variety (*Baeitis rhodani*)—and the Mary-Rambo looked uncannily lifelike. The fly is almost defined by the style of fishing in this case, and can be used in spite of the natural being present rather than because of it. Mind you, the natural mayfly nymphs will be very active in the high-energy water in which this fly is often used, and the natural nymphs will also be in abundance on the slower reaches, so I am happy to say this is more of a "match the moment" than "match the hatch," and that's as good a philosophy as one is going to get, frankly.

Young English river maestro James Hunt fishes the Mary-Rambo under a buoyant dry fly in the foaming water upstream, a place that exudes promise on the lovely River Wharfe at Bolton Abbey in Yorkshire, U.K.

To a dry fly (optional)

TACKLE
Once more it is the trusty 10 ft (3 m) #4 in which I place my hopes. Floating line, of course—although you will not need much of it. A braided or plaited leader and a 5X tippet—I prefer Stroft. It is the best tippet material I have used to date, for this style of fishing and for most other subsurface applications.

VARIATIONS
By varying the color of the quill body (olive, black, natural, orange, red, and so on) a vast array of insects can be suggested. Altering the color of the bead helps, too. Try a copper or silver, rather than the usual gold.

THOMAS EVAN PRITT

Season: Whenever darker mayflies are emerging

Type of fish: Trout and grayling

SNIPE & PURPLE

So often, I think, we just see the sport of fly fishing as being purely about us—our nation. We forget that it is global and that each country has a degree of lineage and claims to the sport. I have to say, it came as a complete shock to find that Northern Italy had a style of fishing and flies that mirrored, almost to the year, the centuries of Northern U.K. wet fly traditions. I was even more astonished to find myself using flies that were almost identical to the ones I have come to know in the North Country tradition.

DIFFICULTY 3/10

MAKING THE FLY

1 Start with the hook in the vise and attach thread that has been well waxed with cobbler's wax.

2 Select a covert feather from the leading edge of a snipe's wing (the darker covert feathers are at the top and the classic, lighter ones on the underside). I lift the feather with the bodkin, separate, and then either pluck out with my fingers or "pinch" out with smooth-jawed forceps/tweezers.

3 Having placed three to four turns of thread on the shank, tie in the dark snipe feather. This is prepared by gently stroking the fibers back against the stem in reverse manner as shown.

4 Tie the snipe feather in by the tip with one to two turns of thread and trim the tip. If you tie in the feather at this stage it makes the job of finishing very much easier.

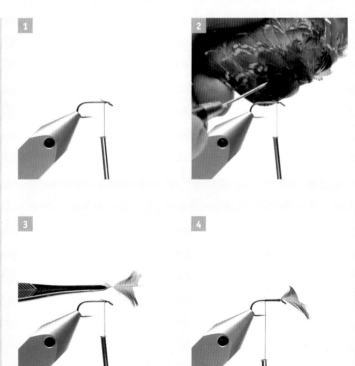

It was, though, fun fishing the Valsesia style crafted in Northern Italy for the boisterous rivers, glacial flowing streams, and bright darting brown and marbled trout with a fixed-length rod of some 16 ft (4.8 m), a length of plaited horsehair line—I kid you not—of about 12 ft (3.6 m) or so, then a leader of about 9 or 10 ft (2.7–3 m) and a team of three or four flies dressed on hooks of about size 16 or 18—the most successful of which had a purple body and a game bird wing! A Snipe (well, probably upland grouse in Italy, and tied a turn or two fuller) and Purple. What fun I had, too! And it far and away outfished all other cunning 21st-century methods as well. It is always said about fishing that you throw out the old and bring in the new at your peril—some nice fishy analogies there.

Hook: Partridge Captain Hamilton dry or Flashpoint dry 14–16
Thread: Purple Gossamer
Hackle: Dark snipe marginal covert feather

MATERIALS

5 Run the thread down the shank to a point opposite the point and then back up the hook shank. Finish the thread wraps just at the back of the hook eye—the turns should be neat and touching and will have swollen marginally around the thoracic area due to covering the clipped hackle.

6 Now, using hackle pliers, create the hackle. Wind the hackle for a maximum of two turns only—do not be tempted to do more. The essence of these patterns lies in the paucity of material.

7 Tie off neatly behind the hook eye and there you have it.

8 May I ever be forgiven for fooling with a classic! Here I offer a variation, with a tiny butt of pearl Mylar, a silver rib, and a morsel of mole dubbing in the thorax. It works very well, proving that even classics can be reinterpreted.

Maintaining a high rod tip angle (as it is here) during the whole fishing phase of spiders is utterly crucial if you are not going to, habitually, miss and lose fish. The angle of the line to the water in that lovely arcing curve is the very epicenter of the method.

TACTICS

The classic method uses a stabilizing fly (a heavier one like the Easy L.D.O. Nymph or a Mary-Rambo or Pheasant Tail Nymph) on the point, then the Snipe and Purple in the middle with another on the top dropper, or a Black Magic—a pattern that is similar and imbues confidence. The key, though, is to find water that will work the patterns. This style is primarily a slightly upstream-across-and-down technique, with the current tensioning the swinging line, and the speed of the river fishing the fly patterns and allowing them to look like a cluster of insects ascending to the surface. Keep the rod at a high angle to the water, allowing the fly line to sweep in a curve to the surface. If you allow the rod and the line to flatten, you will get those short, sharp, on-off "takes" that are so eminently missable.

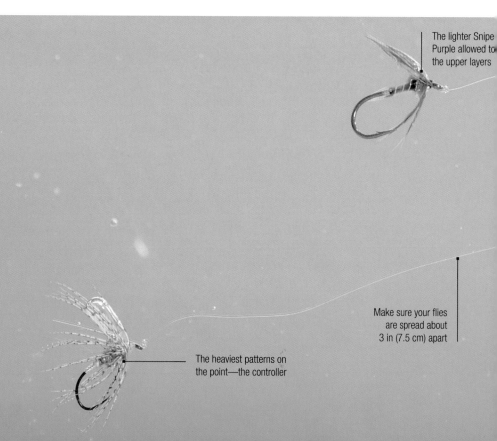

The lighter Snipe Purple allowed to the upper layers

Make sure your flies are spread about 3 in (7.5 cm) apart

The heaviest patterns on the point—the controller

BEHAVIOR

This is the interesting part—it is to me, at least. The seemingly un-insecty form portrayed by the "dry" wet fly becomes utterly transformed when immersed. It becomes a teardrop shape that looks for all the world like a hatching nymph. In the case of the Snipe and Purple, this means the darker mayfly nymphs such as the Iron Blue Dun (in the U.K. and Europe) or the Red Quill and Mahogany Duns and similar darker species in the U.S. But then again, trout and grayling might just like the color scheme. It is, though, a really good choice when you see any darker insect on the water.

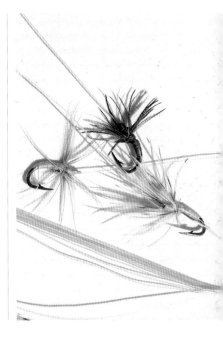

The Italian variations from the Valsesia region, uncannily like North Country spiders and hailing from the same period.

The favorite system

5X/6X tippet

TACKLE

The classic method uses a long fly rod (10 ft [3 m] almost being the minimum), a double tapered line, and a leader of about 12–14 ft (3.6–4.2 m), generally using a 5–6X point and droppers.

VARIATIONS

The pattern shown at the top here—the Snipe & Purple—is the variation previously discussed; the silver rip being an apposite way to suggest the internal hatching fluids and gases of a natural fly. The lower fly is a slightly heavier variation on the Hare's Ear theme—proof that you can adapt classics in a creative and extremely effective way.

THOMAS EVAN PRITT

Season: A pattern to try when emerging mayfly are active.

Designed to suggest Baetis rhodani

Type of fish: Trout and grayling

WATERHEN BLOA

Like any other sphere of life, fly fishing enjoys fads and fashions. For years, the spider—a North Country wet fly type—was almost incarcerated in its northerly home and not really allowed to come out to play on other waters. That was until Sylvester Neames gave the style and patterns prominence through a number of works published in the U.S. Of all the patterns in this genre, this fly is the most versatile and best suited, I believe, to the broad spectrum of mayfly emergence. It is a design I can have faith in.

DIFFICULTY 4/10

MAKING THE FLY

1 With the hook in the vise, take two or three wraps of very well-waxed thread (*see page 11*) and secure in the hook eye area.

2 Attach the hackles as shown, i.e., reverse the fibers and tie in by the tip so that the feather has its dull, or concave, side facing the hook bend. This is so that when wound it will resemble an umbrella shape and envelop the body in an almost teardrop configuration.

3 Continue the thread wraps to a point opposite the hook point.

4 Take the mole fur and separate the short, dense fibers with a dubbing rake—this gives the dubbing air and facilitates sparse dubbing, making the job that little bit easier.

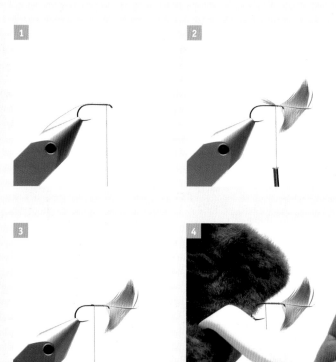

I have had some extraordinary days' sport on this pattern down the years, especially in the U.S. On a recent trip to Arkansas' White River (and what a river that is!) this little design, with the addition of a bead and a little bit of pearl in the body (which I subsequently named the Slim Controller because of its ability to fish other patterns above) literally unraveled some incredibly complex mayfly hatches and provided fishing of near dreamlike quality. It really is a must-have in the fly box.

Hook: Partridge Captain Hamilton dry or Flashpoint dry 14–16

Thread: Well-waxed yellow, yellow-olive, or primrose Gossamer

Dubbing: A very sparse dub of mole or "blue" water rat fur

Hackle: Under-covert or marginal covert from a moorhen's wing—I now use the same feather but coming from a French partridge

MATERIALS

5 Rake a small amount of dubbing as depicted.

6 Now the tricky part: restraint! Dub the mole fur over the waxed thread in such a way that the thread color still glints or peeks through—harder than it first appears!

7 Run this in touching turns to the point where the hackle has been tied in.

8 Wind the hackle for a maximum of two turns, and then finish.

TACTICS

It would be far easier for me to say here, "Well, just follow the instructions and outlines for the Snipe and Purple." Job complete...but we don't want to do that. Instead, I want to urge you to try this style upstream as well. I know of few more effective methods when fish are "bulging" or rising to emergers than this style. The problem that you might encounter is that the point fly sinks the patterns too deeply. I have no hesitation then in reducing the number of flies on the leader to two, taking off the heavy point fly and just having two Bloas—one slightly larger and tied on a heavier hook on the point to turn the system over, and the smaller top fly on the dropper "greased" to float in the surface film.

Steve Patterson, a leading figure in the U.K. Hardy Fly-Fishing Academy, holds a team of soft-hackled flies in the current by maintaining a high rod angle; even at the end of the cast and the flies are in the fished-out position.

Always place the heaviest fly on the point to ensure good turnover and proper fishing depth

BEHAVIOR

There is a point in many an insect's life—and we have talked of this elsewhere in the book—when it finds the quantum leap of breaking through the surface film from the underside next to impossible. Many just get trapped. The wet fly, or soft hackle, is possibly the best imitator of this stage yet devised. Certainly it conveys a very complicated story with simplicity and deft cunning. The Waterhen Bloa is also a perfect imitation of the ascendant nymphs drifting to the surface toward bewinged adult glory. But that is not all. Many *Baetidae* species, when laying eggs in their final spinner (imago) stage, actually do so underwater and look very crumpled as a result. Enter this pattern, too. What a fly!

A rainbow trout hovers just under the surface of this western U.S. river, ready to seize on any passing food form. This is the classic situation for using patterns like wet flies (soft hackles).

e dropper length should be
ut 4–6 in (10–15 cm)

The total leader length should be about 10–14 ft (3–4.5 m)

TACKLE

A long fly rod (10 ft [3 m] almost being the minimum), a double tapered line, and a leader of about 12–14 ft (3.6–4.2 m), generally using a 5–6X point and droppers.

VARIATIONS

I have taken liberties with a classic and concocted one with a pearl "tag" and tiny bead at the head. I call this the Slim Controller.

CHARLES JARDINE

Season: Use any time that you see olive mayflies on the water and trout are seen to be rising to them
Type of fish: Primarily trout, occasionally grayling

DUCK'S DUN

Is it the ultimate vanity to include your own patterns? I suspect that it is, but this one has endured. It has caught fish all over the world, in still and running water, for a very long period, and actually *deserves* its place in the book. Of course, as is always the way, there is nothing startlingly new in this design. Instead, it is a fusion of ideas—and a different twist! Let me explain...

DIFFICULTY 5/10

MAKING THE FLY

1 Place the hook in the vise, wrap a layer of thread, and catch in the tailing materials halfway down the shank.

2 Dub the body in the usual way, finishing approximately two-thirds of the way along the shank: try to make this as segmented, neat, and tapered as you can.

3 Attach the hackle right where you finished the abdominal dubbing.

4 Pair the two CDC feathers in the manner shown so that there is a definite outward curve. Tie these in on top of the shank with a soft loop in the pinch-and-loop style that you would use when constructing a quill wing (*see page 18*). Secure with thread wraps.

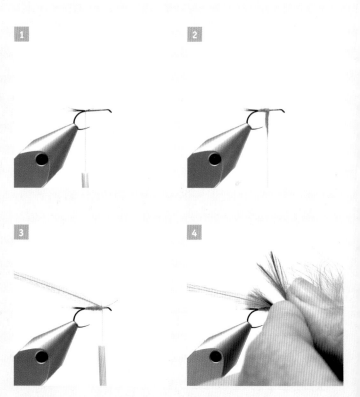

I was fishing as a guest of the late Alan Bramley of Partridge and river maestro John Goddard with Roman Moser on his Austrian Traun in 1986. It was to be a seminal trip. It would be the first time I saw gold beads used in conjunction with a fly, advanced caddis styles, braided leaders with weight in them...and CDC! I immediately took to the feather. No one told me about its flotation attributes. I just liked the structure. At the time I was also looking for a general purpose adult olive (mayfly) pattern that would take the place of the ever-expanding range of patterns spewing from every corner of the fly box. After looking at just about every aspect of the natural, the CDC feathers placed back to back looked like just the thing to me, and so the Duck's Dun, as you see it here, emerged.

Hook: Dry fly 14–20 or TMC 103 BL 15–21

Thread: Claret, olive, or primrose yellow 8/0

Tail: 4–5 saddle cape fibers of jungle cock or hen grizzly fibers

Body: Soft animal fur dubbing—beaver, rabbit under-fur, possum, etc. in colors to match your species

Hackle: Blue dun cock hackle singed underneath with an ophthalmic element or trimmed

Wing: 2 CDC feathers back to back

Thorax: Dubbing, a tone or two darker

MATERIALS

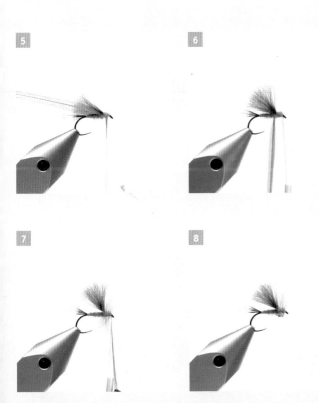

5 Dub the thorax.

6 Take one locating turn of hackle at the back of the wing. This will "set" the wing in an upright manner as shown.

7 Now take the rest of the hackle turns through the thoracic area in an open yet even spiral and tie off.

8 This shows the underside of the hackle singed and ready to fish.

Note: Tailing—the actual material from the jungle cock saddle feather might be easier obtained if you know a traditional salmon fly tier who primarily uses the "eye" feather and not the actual feather.

Noted eastern fly fisher Tom Baltz casts a delicate line and a tiny olive dry fly to fish feeding under a canopy of trees in early morning light on the Yellow Breeches. A lovely time of day for angler, fly, and trout.

TACTICS

The purpose of this pattern was to meet the demands of rising trout during a hatch of upwing mayflies, and so the tactics are largely dictated by this. Of course, there are many ways to approach fish rising in this manner. Several U.S. anglers favor a downstream approach. Personally, I think it papers over the cracks of presentation and places you in full view of the fish. I think it is far better, if you can, to approach on the quarry's blind side from a downstream position and cast up to it or, better still, from a position opposite. Casting across to the quarry also affords better accuracy, offers the fish fewer obvious signs of leader or tippet, and results in more hookups. Fish this pattern during a hatch, matching both size and color as closely as you can, and fish it as drag-free as possible on a light and long tippet.

High wings visible to trout and angler

Footprint from the "singed" hackle

The sunken tippet; the secret to successful dry fly fishing

BEHAVIOR

When you set about imitating nature, you have to be very aware of what it is you actually want to achieve. Tease out the salient points, at least the ones you feel matter to you personally. However, just like with painting, you first need to have something of substance to go on; in this case, the actual insect. This is how this fly came about, through bankside observation of freshly emerged duns of various species conducted over the course of several seasons—capturing, analyzing, and reflecting, and then trying a whole bunch of patterns that just didn't work. That's the way it is. The road is long, but the journey did end at this particular door—the Duck's Dun—and as a freshly emerged adult, gripped to the surface, drying its wings, it has done everything I have asked of it...and more.

*A Small Spurwing (*Centroptilum luteolum*), a lovely little U.K. member of the* Baetidae *family, is just one example of the dun stage that this pattern was designed to match.*

TACKLE
Personally, I would not veer from my trusty 10 ft (3 m) #4, but realistically a 9 ft (2.7 m) or even 8 ft 6 in (2.6 m) #4 rod might be a more obvious choice. When dry fly fishing, I do like somber fly lines—grays, olives, tans—floating naturally. I like long leaders, too. Wherever practicable I use 12–15 ft (3.6–4.5 m) and I recommend the knotted tapered designs popularized by Pennsylvanian fly fishers. Their presentation capabilities are just awesome. I match my tippet to the fly size.

VARIATIONS
None, except for body color and hook size.

THE STIMULATOR

This pattern must be one of the most versatile in use today. The first choice for many western river guides when they need a general pattern for high summer use and to hold a smaller nymph pattern immediately below the surface in turbulent water, this Randall Kaufmann design has found favor throughout the world—even, as strange as this might at first appear to be, on the great lakes—sorry, loughs—of Ireland. It is one of those "all faith" patterns like the Royal Wulff, but with a little more of the "real" about it.

RANDALL KAUFMANN

Season: *Whenever hoppers, light-colored stoneflies, or large caddis are to be imitated*
Type of fish: *Trout of all types (occasionally salmon, too)*

DIFFICULTY 7/10

MAKING THE FLY

1 Offer up the thread and run this down the shank to a point just before the hook bend.

2 Return the thread to the eye of the hook. Tap into alignment 10 to 15 elk fibers, having first prepared them by removing the under-fur with a pet comb. Take an initial firm wrap of thread around the tailing material and then take the thread in ever-decreasing pressure wraps to the start of the hook bend.

3 Tie in the wire rib at this stage.

4 Dub the body with the Antron blend and add the body hackle.

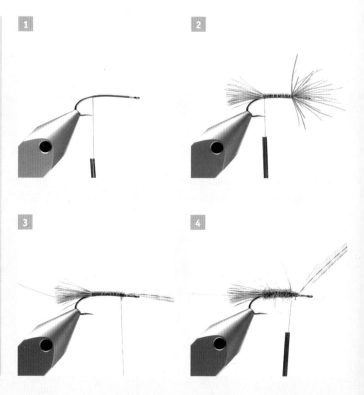

With typical modesty, Randall Kaufmann in his book *Tying Dry Flies* claims that it is "not unique...I have borrowed it, incorporated some of my favorite materials and color combinations and subtly improved on tying style..." I bet the trout wish he hadn't! The great thing about the Stim' is it conveys so much with a minimum of materials and then fishes so well in a wide range of circumstances. For me, it conveys the heat of a Montana summer. Through the parched landscape winds the Madison. You toss a leader holding a size 10, or 8, Stim' with a little Flashback Pheasant Tail or something similar beneath it and pick your way up through the ice-cold water. You lift, and a great slash of flank writhes subsurface. It is the essence of fishing the West, and why it draws anglers to it...and to the Stim'.

Hook: TMC 200 R 4–16

Thread: Orange (flame) 6/0–8/0

Tail: Yearling elk

Rib: Gold wire (fine to medium, depending on fly size)

Body: Bright yellow Antron or Haretron mix

Hackle 1: Ginger cree saddle

Wing: Natural yearling elk

Hackle 2: Grizzly saddle hackle

Thorax: Amber/orange dubbing

MATERIALS

5 Palmer the hackle down the shank and then counter rib with the wire.

6 Add the elk hair wing, preparing it in the same way as the tail, and follow the directions used for the Elk Hair Caddis (*see pages 60–63*). Ensure the wing reaches beyond the bend of the hook. Add the thorax hackle at this stage.

7 Dub the head region with either orange or amber.

8 Wind the hackle in close, yet open, turns through the thorax.

TACTICS

Having already outlined my favorite style of fishing this fly, it may seem superfluous to discuss others, yet this is the essence of the pattern—its ability to meet a wide range of dry fly situations and conquer them. Take, for instance, the loughs of Ireland; not a natural home for a partial giant golden stonefly pattern from the western U.S., yet at mayfly time (*E. danica* and *vulgata*) some local anglers swear by this pattern, fished static and dry or as a top dropper, to move a great deal of water in a big wave. For me, though, this pattern is for boulder-strewn rivers full of riffles and runs and fast-feeding and rising trout—where you can cast it with or without a nymph attached by a thread of tippet to the bend.

A drift boat, a channel of fast water, a western U.S. river in high summer—in this case, the South Fork of Snake—and you have the perfect situation to fish a Stimulator.

The confusion at the surface is similar to a natural large bug

The tail also supports the overall buoyancy

BEHAVIOR

Like many of the designs in this book, this pattern, rather than representing a specific fly or stage, is meant to accommodate a variety of trout foods and insect forms. In Kaufmann's words, it is "a multi-imitator." The list includes caddis, stonefly (especially the *Isoperla* and *Acroneuria* species), and (with a color change) the larger black salmon flies *Pteronarcys californica*, *dorsata*, and others. As a caddis pattern it can cover all manner of species; it is also a great general-purpose grasshopper pattern. Then there is always the fact that trout might just simply like it!

A newly emerged salmon fly, Pteronarcys californica *(or the later emerging* Acorneuria*), is a perfect candidate, when blown onto the water, to be imitated with a darker version of the Stimulator. The light Stim' is a sublime design for the lighter golden* Acorneuria*.*

TACKLE

There is no getting away from the fact that big flies need heavier stuff to propel them. I would definitely recommend for this style of fishing a 9 ft or 9 ft 6 in (2.7–2.8 m) #6 rod and a steeply tapered, slightly shorter leader (9–10 ft [2.7–3 m] is perfect to 4X) to effect a better turnover of this comparatively bulky fly.

VARIATIONS

Try a black version or a golden olive for stone and caddis flies, and an olive version for *E. danica* and *vulgata* when mayflies are hatching.

CHARLES JARDINE AFTER AL TROTH

Season: *When trout are seen to be rising to the surface-oriented natural fly—hatching or spent (this can be almost any point of the fly-fishing season)*

Type of fish: *Trout and grayling*

THE GLITTER (AKA TWINKLE) GULPER

I have always been in awe of Al Troth. There was just something about his fly tying and his philosophies that resonated with me. The first time I came across his fly tying was in a little brochure of his patterns brought back to the U.K. by my mentor Dermot Wilson, who had just fished with him on the Beaverhead. I was smitten. This pattern is directly in tribute to the man. All I have done is add and tweak a little—the essence of the pattern is all Troth.

DIFFICULTY **6/10**

MAKING THE FLY

1 With the hook in the vise, make thread wraps in touching turns in the thoracic area. Offer up the wing post by bringing a section of Antron from the underside of the hook and folding it up into an almost vertical position above. Secure this with wraps on either side and circle the thread around the post to bring the strands together.

2 Tie in the stem of grizzly hackle, having stripped away the webby fiber at the base to reveal the barbules' "sweet-spot." Leave enough of a stem to run up the post so you don't trap the fibers.

3 Circle and run the thread wraps up the post, bringing together the Antron strands and the hackle stem.

4 Run the thread back down the post and along to the hook bend. Place a very small ball of dubbing at the bend and return the thread to where you trimmed the hackle stalk. Tie in

The original Gulper came about through the fish in Hebgen, Henry's, and other lakes in the Montana region that through the summer would dine in relish at the surface on a natural fly known as *Calibaetis,* or speckle-winged quill. The noise the trout made when vacuuming up this pinioned cargo was a very audible slurping sound, hence "gulping." I have had some excellent fishing on English reservoirs with this pattern when the trout have been feeding on midges. So why do so few U.K. anglers fish small on these big lakes? Trout are used to sifting through small fare, yet the English, and to some extent Welsh and Scottish anglers, see anything smaller than size 12 as tiny. Someone really should tell these anglers that the trout never learn hook sizes or a numbering system.

Hook: Down-eye dry fly 12–20
Thread: Claret or orange 8/0 micro
Wing: Orange Twinkle or crystal hair
Hackle: Grizzly saddle or neck
Tail: Clear/white/transparent nylon paint brush fibers—or Microfibetts
Body: Gray animal dubbing—muskrat, rabbit under-fur, etc.

MATERIALS

the tailing materials, ensuring they "hit" the dubbing ball and flare outward like outriggers.

5 With soft gray animal under-fur (or sub) dub the body and the thoracic area around the post. Make a small "mound" of dubbing around the post, to make tying off the hackle easier.

6 Gripping the hackle tip with suitable pliers, carefully run the turns of hackle around the post in touching turns going down the post to the thorax. Secure with a minimum of thread wraps on the hook-eye side of the dubbing shoulder.

7 Add a bit more dubbing, if needed, between the thorax and the hook eye, and whip finish. If required, trim the wing into a shape reminiscent of a mayfly wing.

8 The completed fly.

TACTICS

While I realize this section is about river patterns, I would just like to mention this fly in the context of lake fishing. Oddly enough, there is a bearing here on river fishing in that it is all about "leading" the quarry. Whether you are fishing a running or stillwater, your ability to "read" a rise form can often dictate success. Trying to gauge how far ahead of the last rise form to cast is a question over which we have wrestled and agonized for years. There is no substitute for plain watching rather than casting. I would urge anyone presented with rising trout, especially those fixated on surface food, to have a really good look before pitching their fly toward the area that they assume is the right place; often it's not.

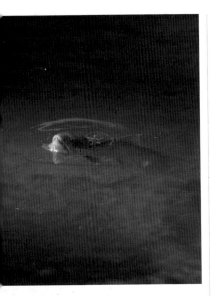

A fly truly gulped! Proof that trout do make the effort.

Why a wing is so important!

The supporting hackle

The trout's eye view

BEHAVIOR

Gulping is a phenomenon not purely confined to lakes. There are many times throughout the course of the season that the audible sound of feeding will direct you to the quarry, and this is just as prevalent on rivers. On lakes, where there is not the same degree of current to dictate a fish's position, one of the key and frustrating traits in this feeding behavior is the way that trout will take a pretty haphazard route in the act of feeding. The angler is left with little choice other than to second-guess the next move. The comfort for the angler lies in the fact that the fish are holding and swimming near the surface, and tend to make regular and multiple rises, rather that just the odd, random one. You can at least plot some sort of course.

The high wing and low profile are the key elements to the Glitter Gulper.

TACKLE
If I had an option, and I fully realize that not everyone will have the luxury of having an outfit to meet every situation, I would opt for a 9 ft or 9 ft 6 in (2.7–2.8 m) #5 rod for this style of fishing. The reasons are its speed in the air and its accuracy. This is also why I would use a steeply tapered leader—knotless on lakes and knotted on rivers (see Humphries or Harvey styles of leaders).

VARIATIONS
None, although you can change the wing-post material to suit conditions.

CHARLES JARDINE

Season: Use this design whenever you see trout feeding on the spent fly on the surface.
Type of fish: Trout

SUNSET SPINNER

At a time when I was in daily contact with streams, anglers, and trout, a book came out called *The Trout and the Fly*, written by Brian Clarke and John Goddard. One area truly changed how I saw flies—the images seen from the fish's point of view. Suddenly all sorts of things made sense, but it was the image of spinners—the last stage of the mayfly's life—taken in evening light that really fueled my passion to delve deeper. Years later, after many false starts, this pattern finally materialized.

DIFFICULTY 6/10

MAKING THE FLY

1 With the hook in the vise, add a layer of thread in the thoracic area and then cross in the wing material. Secure the wing in a spent position as shown, with several firm figure-of-eight turns of thread.

2 Taking a turn or two in a circular fashion around the base of the wing will improve the structure and the silhouette of the wing while also giving the wing stability.

3 Take the thread to the bend of the hook and form a tiny ball of dubbing right on the hook bend.

4 Attach one or two fibers of tailing materials each side. Run the thread over these tails, jamming them against the small nodule of dubbing at the bend, and ensure that they flair outward like outriggers.

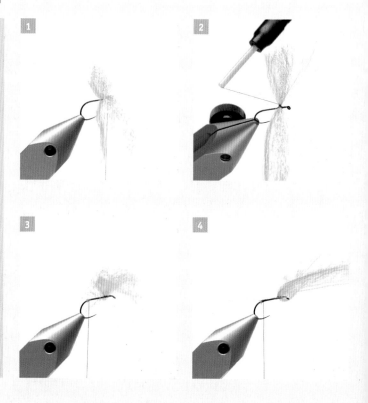

The problem was that when spinners descend on water and lay their precious cargo, they tend to do so *en masse*. So many options for the trout! How is your fly going to be accepted amid hundreds or even thousands of similar naturals? The clue lay in the Clarke and Goddard image. Each spinner was imbued with a halation of light around it. This allowed the last rays of light—usually the orange/red tones, which trout tend to see most easily—to burst around it. Further investigation suggested that orange and red were significant throughout the history of this type of fishing—red spinners predominated. All I did was push the color so that my fly stood out from the crowd and got noticed.

Hook: DE dry fly hook 12–20

Thread: Claret or red 8/0

Wing: Polypropylene in two sections—one clear/white, the other fluorescent flame red

Thorax cover: White Polycellon or Ethafoam strip

Tail: Clear/white paintbrush fibers or Microfibetts

Body: Mixed soft Antron or animal fur dubbing (beaver, etc.) in red and orange 50/50 mixture

MATERIALS

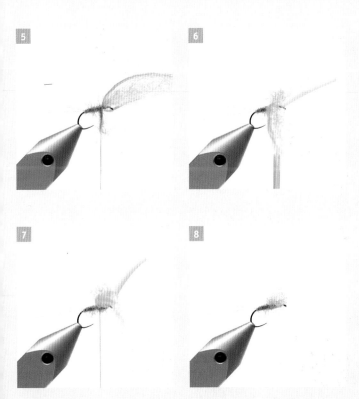

5 Run the dubbing to the wing.

6 Now comes the cunning part: add a sliver of white foam through the wing on the top side in an advanced manner so that it faces over the eye.

7 Dub the thoracic area. I use the same dubbing as the body; you might want to try a darker one. Be careful to cover the areas around the wings, but also take care not to make the thorax too chunky. Keep the thread to the rear of the thorax as depicted.

8 Bring the foam back and through the wings. Secure at the rear of the thorax with three wraps at most and finish at this point. Trim the wings as shown and you are done.

TACTICS

 A heavy fall of spinners is a wonder to behold: the air and the water are suddenly painted with little fragile orbs of natural fleeting light. However, given such a natural multitude, the angler is often left grasping for any clue or metaphorical tactical straw to clutch onto. Observation and accuracy are key: spotting a regularly feeding trout; deducing whether it's taking every fly or is feeding in sequence; ascertaining the right size of the chosen species and then matching it with a suitably sized Sunset; and finally casting accurately to the quarry.

BEHAVIOR

A multitude of spinners can be an awesome sight, but more often we are talking little flurries and pockets of fly, rather than vast armadas. The aspect that trout find so beguiling with this pattern is that it's not going anywhere. Worn out through her egg-laying exertions, the spinner is gripped in the surface film and just waits for her short life to finally run out. At this point the wings are usually flat in the surface and at right angles to the body. Knowing the food item is not going to suddenly dart away ensures that the trout can feed in a leisurely and selective manner.

The aspect conveying the last stage of an upwing's life

The wing color is highly visible to the trout and the fisher

TACKLE

Because of the accuracy aspect of this type of fishing I tend to favor a 9 ft or 8 ft 6 in (2.7–2.55 m) rod as opposed to a longer one—the shorter rod is much faster through the air. I would advise the knotted style of tapered leader for critical turnover, and use a tippet as fine as you can get away with, given the hook size. De-grease the final foot of leader with mud to take away any vestiges of shine.

VARIATIONS

None, although I occasionally use a bright chartreuse-bodied version. Weird, but productive.

SOME STILLWATER
FAITHFULS

ROB SPILLER

Season: All
Type of fish: Trout

NOMAD

This fly is not for the purist. Insect-based it certainly is not, but no one has told the trout. Over the last ten or more seasons, this pattern has become enshrined in U.K. stillwater fly-fishing folklore. It is a pattern that, when all about you are failing, you can pin some faith on. For an attractor-cum-streamer style of design this fly utilizes a surprisingly small hook, and although I have tried larger variations, the smaller sizes seem to work a lot better. I don't have a clue why, but it means you don't have to sacrifice your light-line values to fish it.

DIFFICULTY 5/10

MAKING THE FLY

1 Select a bead that will actually go round the hook bend. I prefer the purpose-designed "slit" beads. It is also worth tying some in brass and some in the heavier tungsten.

2 Attach the chartreuse floss and craft an even-tapered layer, periodically checking to see where the bead stops and jams along the shank.

3 Maintain the layers until you get a smooth, even, cigarlike taper. Tie off the floss with a whip finish.

4 Jam the bead in place, apply a layer of five-minute epoxy to the head area, and then set aside to dry thoroughly (I allow 24 hours). I also work in batches.

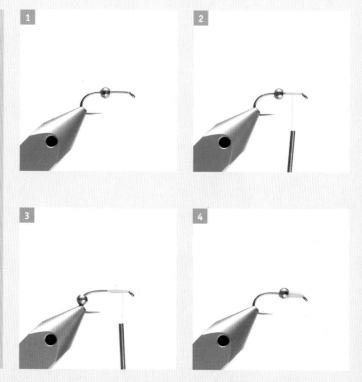

I suppose you could imagine it as being a leech—but with a chartreuse head?! The other surprising thing about the fly is not just that it seems to attract better than average-sized fish—which it does—but the construction of the pattern ensures an even rate of descent that seems to be deadly in its own right. I have also tried this pattern on rivers, where it hasn't done that well. I am not sure why, but perhaps it is the lack of actual bulk. However, for stillwater it is truly deadly; if you are in a tricky situation, tie one on. Curiously, it is surprising just how many "fallen angels" I see along our river and lake banks!

Hook: Standard wet 10–12 threaded with a gold brass or tungsten bead of appropriate size

Thread: Head, Glo Brite chartreuse floss

Body: Black 8/0

Tail: Black marabou. Black/peacock micro cactus chenille

MATERIALS

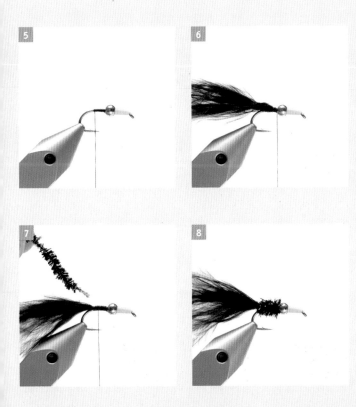

5 Attach some black thread and place a layer along the rear half of the shank.

6 Immediately behind the bead, tie in a plume of marabou fibers.

7 Run the thread down the shank in very close touching turns, trapping the marabou as you proceed. Then, at the bend, tie in the chenille, having first exposed the core so as not to get any unsightly buildup.

8 Return the thread to just behind the bead and wind the chenille in very close turns. On reaching the bead, tie off and whip finish at this point.

TACTICS

Given that this is a stillwater design, it will accommodate most styles—whether you are fishing a sunken line or not. My preferred choice, however, is to use a long leader of 18 to 25 ft (5.5–7.6 m) in conjunction with a floating line. Cast out in a promising area, let the line be bowed into an arc by the surface push and wave action, and then just hand twist to keep up with the slowly arching line, leader, and fly. Alternatively, you can use this pattern as a point fly when fishing a team of nymphs when either float tubing or boat fishing (drifting in the time-honored way and casting to the front of the boat: *see traditional loch-style fishing, page 210*). In any event, it is a design that likes to be fished pedantically!

Blithfield Reservoir, in the heart of the English Midlands, is an ideal place, especially during early spring, to use black-and-green patterns like the Nomad.

The fluorescent chartreuse head makes the fly very visibl

The bead midships ensures an even sink rate

The long marabou tail just pulses with life

BEHAVIOR

I guess that we have pretty much covered this area, but by virtue of the bead being in the middle of the design, this will ultimately ensure an evenness of descent, a factor that so often accounts for its success and, I believe, the reason why trout, on many occasions, take this fly—purely because it sinks evenly, under its own volition. The marabou tail also adds to the effectiveness and lithe action: one small tweak and the fly just seems to have a mind and motion all its own. Please don't be tempted to reduce the tail length, because you will reduce the effectiveness by the same degree. The pattern is more for the open water and simply does not respond to being fished too quickly.

The legendary English stillwater specialist John Wadham lands an early-season rainbow in hostile conditions. John has used patterns like this Nomad to catch pike, perch, chub, salmon, and, of course, trout.

TACKLE
I prefer a 9 to 10 ft (2.7–3 m) rod, taking either a #6 or #7 line. As I have said, a floating line is the way to go with this pattern and I will "grease" up the tip to ensure the line "rides high." Pay careful attention to the leader setup. I use either a 12 or 15 ft (3.6–4.5 m) knotless tapered leader to about 3X or 4X, then tie in one of those tiny stainless steel rings, and then add a further tippet in fluorocarbon in a similar size—or a diameter to match the situation and/or fly size.

VARIATIONS
Well, these are color combinations more than variations:
- yellow/chartreuse head with a pearl chenille body and white tail works well; pink head, pearl body, and white tail
- red head, olive body, and olive tail
- all white
- all black

and so on—let your imagination run wild. What have you got to lose?

CHARLES JARDINE

Season: Damsel nymphs are available to trout throughout the year, but be aware of color changes: light in winter, tending to darken toward summer
Type of fish: *Primarily trout but it has caught bass and panfish*

DOWN & DIRTY DAMSEL

It's funny how a set of circumstances can create a truly good pattern. A form of "Cometh the hour, cometh the fly," to paraphrase. That is the case here. Years ago, when fishing in legendary rock singer Roger Daltrey's delightful lakes at Lakedown in Sussex in the South of England, we were presented with a problem, and this fly came into being as the solution to that problem.

DIFFICULTY 5/10

MAKING THE FLY

1 With the hook in the vise and the eyes tied in on a base of thread with figure-of-eight wraps followed by a "smear" of instant glue, tie in the marabou plumes.

2 Return the thread to the halfway stage, fold a strand of Crystal Hair around the thread, and "tie in" so that a strand lies on either side of the tail.

3 Tie in the hackle just behind the eye; tying it in now will give you far more working space later.

4 Return the thread to the hook bend (if you want to rib the pattern you can add the rib now) and start to dub the body using a noodle or rope style of dubbing. This will ensure a firm, segmented, "tight" body.

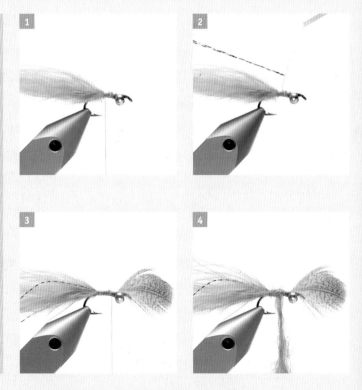

One particular lake was designated as a "floating line only" water. We realized that if we wanted to catch the better-than-average fish that patrolled and hunted the deeper layers, we would have to alter our fly designs to meet the depth and the discerning palette of the larger spotted inhabitants. Sheer weight was not the answer; we needed a design that was suggestive of a lithe and athletic damsel nymph—sparse, but heavy enough to descend. I reasoned that the only bulbous area of the fly was the head and eye region, so that was where I placed the weight. Man, did it work! OK, it follows a path well trodden by the likes of Dave Whitlock, Peter Cockwill, and so on, but the melding of the various materials and action in this one design has proved to be a revelation. I don't leave home without it.

Hook: Standard wet 10–12 with the addition of presentation brass eyes or lead eyes tied in on the underside

Thread: Light–dark olive 8/0

Tail: Long marabou plume in various olive tones to match the species and time of year. Flanked by a strand of Twinkle or Crystal Hair in blue

Rib: Optional—medium to fine oval gold tinsel

Body: Mixed animal fur dubbing: rabbit dubbing, or mohair blends to match the olive tones of the natural

Hackle: Olive dyed partridge

Thorax pad: 4–5 strands of olive Crystal Hair

Thorax: As for body, only a shade or two darker

MATERIALS

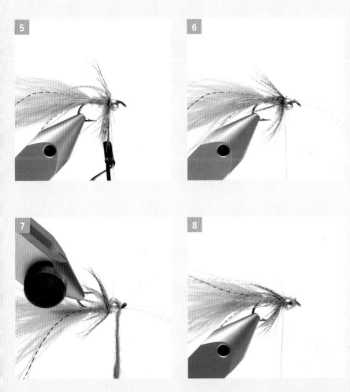

5 Wind the hackle—about one-and-a-half to two turns will do it.

6 Add the Crystal Hair strand wing pads with turns of thread so that they project fore and aft—back over the bend and over the hook eye.

7 Return the thread to just short of the hackle, invert the hook in the vise, and dub the thoracic area, ensuring that the dubbing covers the thread turns securing the eyes.

8 Return the hook to the upright position, bring the forward-projecting Crystal Hair strands back to where the hackle is secured, and whip finish on the hook bend side of the eyes.

Float tubing the lakes in the western U.S. can be very productive with damsel patterns, especially when fished near weed beds and spring activity.

TACTICS

The design is calculated to resemble the nymphal form of a damsel fly, so this should dictate your tactics. However (and seemingly few fly fishers realize this), the damsel nymph can, where it occurs, be at the mercy of attentive lake trout for a good eight months of the year—hence the color and size range. The smaller juveniles tend to be a washed-out, yellow-olive color that progressively darkens as the insect grows into maturity and impending adulthood at the surface—and beyond. This all goes on in and around weed beds, which is, of course, where you should concentrate your efforts. Mostly these are the shallower areas of lakes and reservoirs, but given the movement and color scheme that just seems to prove a fatal attraction for trout, you can quite confidently fish this pattern almost anywhere.

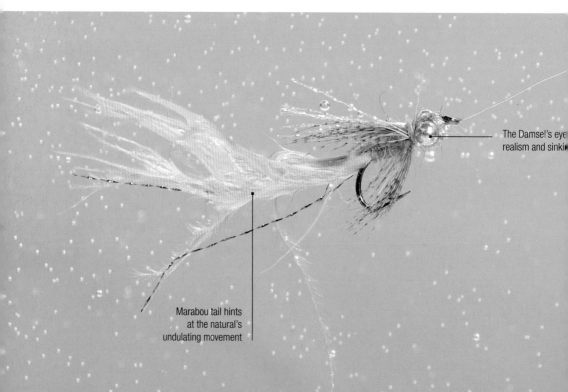

The Damsel's eye realism and sinki▶

Marabou tail hints at the natural's undulating movement

BEHAVIOR

The tail is the length it is to suggest the undulating wiggle of the natural's abdomen. I am firmly convinced that movement is a key trigger for trout, so the tail is there to seduce the quarry. Your role is to activate the lithe seducer by moving it, and that is done by retrieving the design either in short twitches or with a stuttering, faltering, figure-of-eight twist movements of the line hand. Just experiment. Depth is crucial, and you really want to aim for a band between 2 ft and 8 ft (0.6–2.4 m) down in the water column, which seems to be generally the most productive area. As I mentioned, this concept came about because we had to use floating lines, but it works wonderfully well on intermediates and type 3 sinking lines—and on sink tips, too, especially the new generation clear tips.

This is the caliber of rainbow trout that aggressively hunts down both natural damsel nymphs and their imitators.

TACKLE

A 9–10 ft (2.7–3 m) rod is perfect, taking a #6 or even #7 line. That's on the heavy side, I know, but this is a weighty fly and very often there will be a need to "go the distance." If you are using a floating line, you will need to use a long leader (18–20 ft [5.5–6 m] plus is ideal). Of course, for sinking lines 12 ft (3.6 m) is adequate.

VARIATIONS

The variations come in either the size of hook or the varying colors of olive. I have even tied an all-black version. Worryingly, it worked!

MONTANA NYMPH

I guess everyone has a pattern that is just plain unproductive. Given a seething mass of ravenous trout in a bathtub, I wouldn't catch on this pattern. I have tried, time after time. Nothing. The fly hates me. Mind you, it seems to work the world over for everyone else, especially in the U.K., where the addition of the chartreuse thorax has created a pattern that is the one of choice for many. I really don't know why it won't work for me. And, yes, I do take it personally.

LEW OATMAN

Season: *This pattern is not dependant on a time of year.*
Type of fish: *Trout (although many coarse fish have been taken on this design in the U.K.)*

DIFFICULTY 5/10

MAKING THE FLY

1 With the hook in the vise, run the thread down the shank, and between a third and half way down catch and tie a cluster of black cock hackle fibers (about eight to ten).

2 Add the lead wire in and around the thoracic area, followed by, if desired, the rib.

3 Strip the fiber from the core of the chenille and tie in this core. This will lead to far less buildup on the body and the resultant dressing.

4 Having wound the chenille up two-thirds of the body and ribbed the area, add two strands of chenille for the thorax pad.

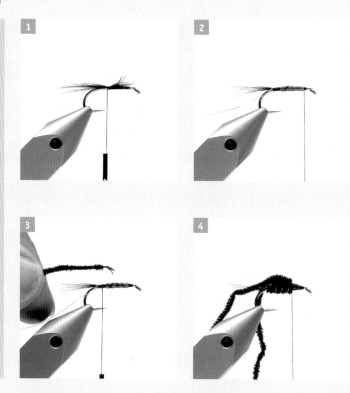

That said, the U.K. version (the one depicted) is actually a long way from the original that was designed to be an impressionistic representation of the giant black stonefly—the salmon fly—*Pteronarcys californica*—found predominantly in the Western U.S. Actually, kindred species can be found the world over where you have rough-and-tumble streams and chaotic flows—and trout love 'em. But, of course, it is a very unlikely "hatch" on English reservoirs such as Rutland, Grafham, or Blagdon. The black and bright greeny yellow is just a combination that seems to work and trigger trout, be they brown or rainbow, and, oddly, other unrelated species, too. Pike, perch, chub—a whole mass of species seem to fall for this color combination's charms.

Hook: Standard wet 8–12. Long shank 8–12 weighted with lead wire as desired

Thread: Black 8/0

Tail: 8–10 cock hackle fibers

Rib: Oval silver tinsel (medium)

Body: Black chenille (base the size of chenille on the size of hook)

Thorax pad: Black chenille

Thorax: Classic; yellow chenille. U.K. favorite; chartreuse chenille

Hackle: Black cock hackle

MATERIALS

5 Now add the chartreuse chenille in the same way, stripped to the core, and then the black cock hackle.

6 Wind the chartreuse chenille thorax. You must take care here. Chenille is bulky; be careful with the turns and finish a little shorter of the hook eye than normal.

7 Palmer the thoracic area with the cock hackle and tie off at the eye—this is why you need room in this area.

8 Pull the strands of black chenille over the thoracic area, secure at the eye, and whip finish—a further reason why you require ample room at the hook eye.

197

TACTICS

I am truly tempted to say, "Don't ask me!" but instead I have asked a friend. The response seems to be, "Just add water... and hang on." Well, you need a little more than that, don't you? On its home waters it is fished "dead drift" in heavy flows and as near to the riverbed as practical, but on stillwaters it would seem that it can be fished on just about any line type and at any depth where one might realistically expect the fish to be. One friend, stillwater legend John Wadham, uses this pattern as an "anchor" to support some smaller nymphs above on a floating line and long leader setup. It is a scenario that works for me—but with a similarly colored Nomad as opposed to a Montana on the point. C'est la vie.

What can be said for the boat fisher is equally true for the bank fisher. The Montana Nymph has become one of the leading fish takers at all depths on U.K. stillwaters.

The chenille body's bulk looks "buggy"

The hackle gives the fly life but also ensures it does not get fouled up on the bottom

BEHAVIOR

There are definite pros and cons with a design like this. One thing is certain; the inherent quality of chenille lies in its density. The shape is hardly diaphanous, but solid and bulky. This fact alone makes it wonderful for depicting insects of similar structure; but beyond that, especially in cloudy or "stained" water, it ensures that maximum visual contact can be made by the quarry, especially if the pattern is moved slowly. The other thing about chenille is that it absorbs water and therefore, once fully saturated, will sink very quickly—a real advantage when fishing fast streams. However, as a little aside, this water absorption (I am told), when unweighted, allows the fly to drift down through the layers in a very smooth and apparently deadly way, a way trout find hard to resist. Oh, really?

An early-season trout comes to the boat. The Montana Nymph is one of the key patterns for fishing slow and deep at this time of year.

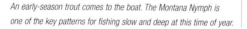

TACKLE

Given the variety of situations this pattern can be used in, the area of gear specific to this design is a tricky one to answer. All I would suggest is to match the outfit to the application—the bigger the fly, the heavier the outfit. In a fast river with a heavily leaded, large, long shank version, a 9 ft (2.7 m) #6 or #7 would be perfect, but for the smaller standard hook versions fished on U.K. stillwaters, a 9 ft or 10 ft (2.7–3 m) #5 is ideal. As ever, match the rod and line to the size of fly as you would the tippet.

VARIATIONS

None. The original had an orange chenille thorax.

SIMON KIDD

Season: All
Type of fish: Trout

DEEP WATER BUZZER

One of the most important aspects of U.K. fishing is imitating and fishing *chironomid* pupae. This aspect is almost a subject in its own right and, oddly, it seems to occupy the thoughts of just U.K. anglers, some Canadian lake fishers, and an increasing number in Europe. Elsewhere, the diverse members of the vast order of dipteran flies—"true flies"— seem to be viewed as imitations from a Lilliputian world and are only tied on the tippet in desperation when trout are feasting on microinsects. Think again!

DIFFICULTY 5/10

MAKING THE FLY

1 Start the thread at the hook eye and offer up the Swiss straw.

2 Tie in both the Swiss straw and the Spanflex with successive turns of thread, stretching and reducing the Spanflex by pulling with your non-winding hand.

3 Continue these touching turns to a point well around the hook bend. Now craft the underbody and take this to a point seven-eighths of the way along the hook shank toward the eye.

4 Bring the Swiss straw over the back, and in very even, near-touching turns take the Spanflex up the shank, relaxing the pressure just a little to create a defined rib over this shell-back.

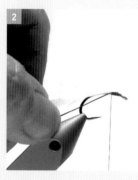

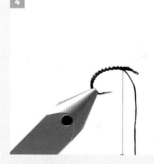

By and large, on reservoirs and lakes you can split the midge species into two distinct types: deep-water loving and shallow-water loving. There does seem to be another little group—and a significant one for the fly fisher—that colonizes almost anywhere there is a buildup of lake bed silt (old ditches, meetings of current lines, where a stream spills into a lake and descends into deeper areas, carrying sedimentary deposits with it). These are the areas loved by bloodworms—the *chironomid* larvae—and, naturally, the resultant pupae. These areas are magnets for the trout and tend to offer larger-than-average natural midges: enter this wonderful design by my old friend Simon Kidd, as exceptional a fisher as ever strung a fly rod.

Hook: Curved grub 6–12

Thread: Black, dark olive, claret, bottle green 8/0 (actually any color that matches the intended species)

Shell-back: Clear raffene (Swiss straw)

Rib: Black, dark green, maroon, etc. medium Spanflex

Body: Under the thread you can add a layer of pearl Mylar for extra sheen

Wing-buds: Fluorescent orange dyed goose biot

Thorax cover: Spanflex

Thorax: Spanflex or buildup of thread

Breathers (optional): White nylon "baby" wool or white Antron

MATERIALS

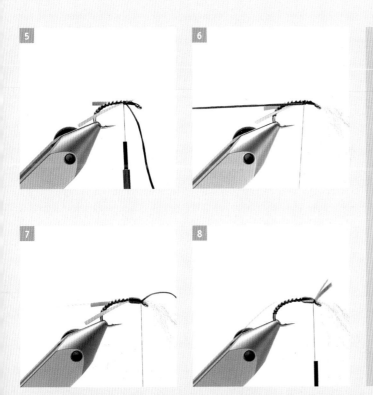

5 Secure and trim the shell-back. Now tie in the goose biots on either side and in the direction shown (angled slightly down toward the hook point).

6 Either secure the original Spanflex in a position that takes it back over the hook or add another section of Spanflex so that it points back toward the bend.

7 Add the breathers and build up the thorax (either with Spanflex or thread wraps), and then bring the thoracic pad over the thorax and secure.

8 Bring the wing pads forward as shown, secure them in this position, and trim. Whip finish and then trim the breathers.

A terrific reservoir rainbow taken on midges.

TACTICS

The actual fishing of the design is based (as a gross oversimplification) on the angler casting this pattern out on the point with a similar (but smaller and lighter) wire hook design above it and the further addition of yet another above that. Even general-purpose patterns such as the Diawl Bach are employed in the supporting role. The fly is allowed to descend to the desired subsurface level and depth, and is then retrieved very slowly with a hand twist. Alternatively, you could just cast out (especially if you are bank fishing) and let the breeze swing the team around under its own volition. Beyond that, the permutations are almost endless, especially if you are fishing from a boat or float tube, where sunk lines in various densities can deliver the pattern in many ways.

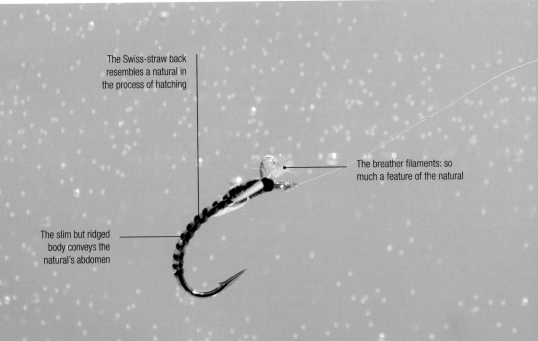

The Swiss-straw back resembles a natural in the process of hatching

The breather filaments: so much a feature of the natural

The slim but ridged body conveys the natural's abdomen

BEHAVIOR

What is often overlooked when examining the world of the nonbiting midge is the natural fly's ability to just "hold" in a certain spot and drift, wind- and current-aided, for quite a long way before hatching. This is why the cast, wait, and slow retrieve across a wind is so successful. Also, because of the fetal shape of the imitation (when tied on a curved hook), it does represent the insect at rest and drifting. This is the clue as to how to fish it—drifting, wind-aided. What I also do is studiously seek out those silt beds I mentioned and fish this style of pattern in those areas. When I use this pattern as an "anchor" pattern to fish other styles of fly above, it is invariably this fly that catches the fish.

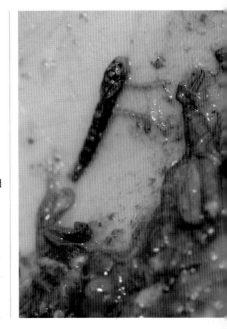

The proof of the pudding—almost literally! The natural midge and accompanying dinner ingredients.

TACKLE
Frankly, the stillwater gear that we have already suggested is perfect. However, I would, if fishing a very long leader, possibly use a 10 ft (3 m) rod rather than one smaller, and a #6 or #7 line to carry the particular payload. When crafting the leaders I take a 12 ft or 15 ft (3.6 or 4.5 m) leader and add this to a 2–4 ft (0.6–1.2 m) butt section that is permanently attached to the fly line; thereafter, I add the tippet or droppers as required below this to fashion the length of leader necessary. This taper is crucial for good turnover, as is the additional rod length.

VARIATIONS
None, apart from changing the body thread color.

VARIOUS

Season: *All, but best in spring through early fall*
Type of fish: *Mostly trout, but many coarse fish also seem to like it!*

DIAWL BACH

If any recent pattern has had a greater impact on the U.K. stillwater scene than this one, I'd love to know its name. The Diawl Bach (a Welsh name meaning, suitably, "Little Devil") has simply taken over as the U.K.'s premier stillwater pattern. I don't have a good reason why—only that it works exceptionally well. Of course, one of the key attributes is its slimness of dressing—sparse patterns catch fish, it is that simple, and when one comes to consider trout and trout fishing, success is reason enough.

DIFFICULTY 4/10

MAKING THE FLY

1 Attach the thread and almost immediately catch in the tail material at the thoracic area.

2 Then, again almost immediately, attach the ribbing material.

3 After that, attach the two strands of peacock herl. If you can find them—and they are rare—select herls with very short fibers.

4 Run the thread in very close and, if possible, touching turns, to hide the previously tied-in materials. In order to enhance this paucity of dressing, add a touch of instant glue along the hook shank and just as it is about to go tacky and set...

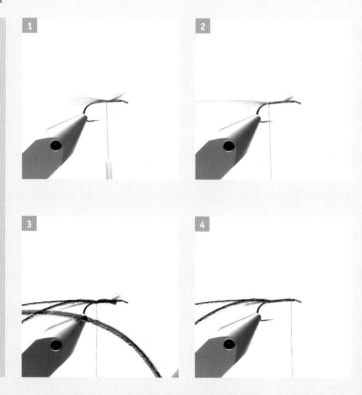

The fact the materials suggest such a diversity of insects is probably the key: it is one of a cluster of rare patterns that convey so many, yet imitate few. For the occasional angler and fly fishers who just want to carry a few "faith" patterns or "near-certainties," patterns like this can restrict the fly box and reduce the angst over selecting the fly *du jour*. This factor alone will often lead to more success, concentrating on the actual fishing of a pattern and not on constant fly changes and appraisal. Actually, the more imitative fisher might be tempted to have a box merely containing Hare's Ears. I have often wondered whether you could cover a season on stillwaters with a box full of variations on Diawl Bach and the Hare's Ear theme, but then where would be the fun in that...or the point of this book!

Hook: Standard wet 10–14 (10 being the most useful overall)

Thread: Claret, black, red, and fluorescent red

Tail: 4–6 fibers of natural red cock hackle

Rib: Pearl Mylar (or copper wire)

Body: Two strands of peacock herl

Hackle: 10 fibers of red cock hackle

Thorax: Red Glo-Brite floss or holographic Mylar (I prefer the Mylar)

MATERIALS

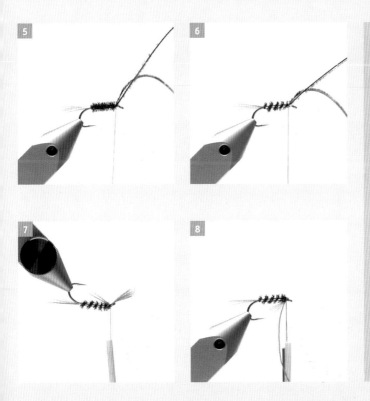

5 ...run the peacock herl in close turns up the shank. Do not twist the fibers to form a rope, but keep them as open as possible to avoid bulk (hence the use of an agent like glue).

6 Rib the design in the same way as the turns of body material, finishing just shy of the hook eye.

7 Invert the hook in the vise and catch in about 10 cock hackle fibers as a beard hackle.

8 Finish with a flourish. Add a red floss head or a red holographic Mylar head followed by the red floss: trout seem to love a hint of red, especially on this design.

A trout succumbs to a Diawl variation.

TACTICS

This pattern is best fished in conjunction with a weightier point fly—the Deep Water Buzzer would be perfect—and then have either one or two designs running up the leader from droppers. If fish are seen near the surface, you might conceivably put another Diawl on the point as well. I would urge you to fish this pattern slowly rather than fast, but as is usual in trout fishing until we find that talking trout we will never have the definitive answer. This pattern, though, is a design in which you can have complete confidence, whether you are fishing in the U.S., Canada, the U.K., Ireland, or any other place where you encounter trout.

The bright red head is a significant trigger to the trout

The pearl or holographic Mylar adds further attraction

BEHAVIOR

OK, the Diawl Bach is one of a cluster of patterns that can be best described as "general" and "impressionistic." That said, the primary function of the design is to suggest the darker nymphs that one might realistically find on a stillwater. The awful truth here—and many trout-fishing students will throw up their collective hands in horror—is that trout really don't know the names of the creatures they are eating! The fact that this pattern suggests dark bugs is enough—be those "bugs" nonbiting midges or whatever. The idea is to cast and fish it, and not to deliberate too much.

Evening cast at Blagdon in Somerset in the U.K. It is often seen as the home of stillwater nymph fishing.

TACKLE
Just about any stillwater gear will do, but my preference would be for a 10 ft (3 m) rod and a #5 line—make it a floater, please, or a Mini Tip or similar clear sink tip. You might find a #7 or #6 line appropriate to the conditions.

VARIATIONS
Adding different-colored ribs—red holographic, pearl, gold, and so on—will give you a world of difference and variety. Also, varying the size and weight of hook will allow you to explore all the opportunities afforded by the various layers and locations where trout hunt.

UNKNOWN

Season: *Best in late spring, summer, and especially fall*
Type of fish: *Predominantly trout, including sea trout, and salmon*

THE RED PALMER

This pattern is uncannily similar to the design that Aelian, the first chronicler of angling, described when he noted that "speckled fishes" of Macedonia were taking "wasplike flies" buzzing on the surface, and he imitated these with a "wattle from a cock." Now there's an image to consider! It certainly seemed to embody the colors here, and that was in about A.D. 200. This is a bit more refined, but the actual design is much the same as the one my great-grandfather would have used. It is an old style—but the trout don't care.

DIFFICULTY 4/10

MAKING THE FLY

1 With the hook secured in the vise, attach the thread in touching turns by the eye and almost immediately "catch in" the wool tailing material.

2 Secure the tail by running the thread in touching turns down the shank, adding the tinsel rib as you go.

3 Taking another piece of wool, open up the ply and separate the strands. Tie in just one of these at the hook bend. Alternatively, use red dubbing.

4 Wind this in a smooth, even manner up the shank—this is very good discipline for other designs, as it will teach you that the underbody must be as smooth as possible if you are to avoid any unsightly "lumps and bumps" along the dressing.

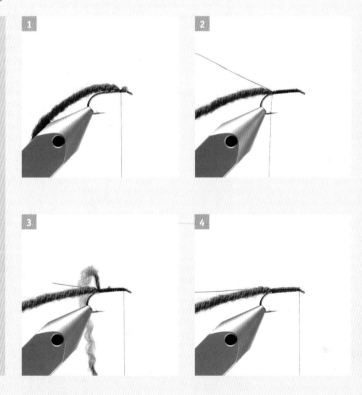

What flies of this generic style convey to me is summer holidays in Scotland, pursuing sea trout and brown trout on windswept lochs and wild, remote burns, the smell of heather and damp bracken. It brings back wonderful memories. I am going to add into the mix another of the classics and an essential bit of Ireland: the Bibio—an impression of the heather fly or bloody doctor, *Bibio marci*. If you learn to construct one or the other of these patterns, a whole world of the "classic" and the "traditional" starts to come into your fly-tying life. This style of tying may have been superseded by cutting-edge designs encompassing every realistic appendage known to man, but this whole gamut of flies has stood the test of time and embodies the charm, hope, and, yes, madness of the sport.

Hook: Standard wet fly 8–14

Thread: Red, claret, brown, or black 6/0–8/0

Tail: Red wool (the knitting type is fine)

Rib: Oval gold

Hackle: Natural brown cock hackle—single for sparse, double for "full"

Body: Red tailing wool or red seal's fur (sub) dubbing

MATERIALS

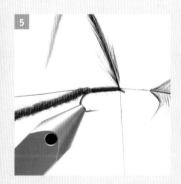

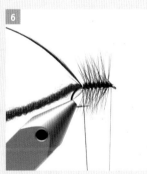

5 Return the thread to the hook eye and tie in one or two cock hackles. If you want a pattern that really pushes water, go for two hackles; if you want a design that copes with calmer days, opt for one. I also prefer a hackle that errs on the soft side rather than the more brittle, generic "dry fly" hackles.

6 Palmer the hackle down the hook shank in even, open turns.

7 Carefully make one or two very firm securing turns with the rib material at the hook bend around the hackle, trapping it securely, then counter rib in an even spiral up the hook shank.

8 For an even bushier design, add a further head hackle. I find one or two are perfect in the majority of situations. Lastly, use varnish to fashion a smooth, neat head.

TACTICS

Having alluded to the "traditional loch style," it's only fair (especially to the American fly fisher and those unfamiliar with the whole concept) to describe what it is. The idea is to fish three or four flies on a leader of appropriate length. This terminal system is then fished on long rods—10 ft (3 m) being normal and 11 ft (3.3 m) not excessive—usually with a floating line (sometimes an intermediate or higher density), to the front of a moving boat, drifting broadside down the wind (and if necessary slowed down by the use of a drogue, a form of subsurface parachute). The system is then cast out and retrieved slightly, or considerably, faster than the boat, depending on the prevailing conditions and the trout's preferences on the day. The idea is to get the flies to rumble and push water just under the surface, the spiral hackle of the palmer creating a fish-attracting wake.

Martin Cottis, the local guide on Bristol's Chew Valley Reservoir in the U.K., and his son, fish in the time-honored broadside-drifting tradition. A place and style that lend themselves to the Red Palmer.

The fly being fished just below the surface and not "on" or "in" the surface film

The palmered hackle "pushing" water

The attractive red "tag" or tail

BEHAVIOR

The Palmer series is really an attractor and not designed to represent anything specific that is natural in the accepted sense. That said, the concept is used to convey a broad spectrum of suggestive ideas to the quarry. Realistically, one might imagine this to be a vague impression of a whole gamut of sedgelike species, especially the larger reddish-tan species, but the design has also accounted for any number of trout feeding on the large red midge, also known colloquially as the "grenadier." A close friend of mine, the great U.K. fly tier Bob Carnill, uses this pattern on Midland reservoirs when trout are harvesting sticklebacks toward the fall—with devastating results. So, as is often the case, the attraction is in the eye of the beholder: in this case, the trout. Your job as the fisher is to breathe life into the inanimate.

Nathan Clayton, manager of the prolific English Midland Reservoir, Pitsford, nets one of its magnificent rainbows taken on a Red Palmer imitating a stickleback (we like to think!).

TACKLE
Use a 10–11 ft (3–3.3 m), #5–#7 rod, matched with a range of floating, intermediate, and type 2 density fly lines. If you have not done this before, you'll also need an inquiring mind, a spirit of adventure, a boat that drifts steadily broadside, and a drogue. Oh—and nerves of steel for when you're eyeball to eyeball with a large wild brown trout about to engulf your Palmer, Bibio, or other classic wet fly from the surface.

VARIATIONS
None, but you sometimes see this pattern tied with a peacock herl body.

VARIOUS

Season: *All*
Type of fish: *Trout—brown and rainbow*

THE QUILL BUZZER

Quill patterns have been around for generations and the reason for this is compelling. It's not just because they work for trout in a large majority of often difficult situations—they do—but the secret lies in two areas, both attendant to the material: lightness and contrast shading. One allows for the fly to be fished where the insect at this stage is most likely to occur, and the other accurately recreates the segmentation. All in all, a fine pair of reasons why you should "tie one on."

DIFFICULTY 5/10

MAKING THE FLY

1 With your hook in the vise, place a very smooth layer of thread along the shank and, at the very extremity of the hook bend, "catch in" the stripped quill by the thicker base, not the fine tip.

2 I then place a very smooth and thin layer of instant glue along the shank. This will support the fragile quill.

3 You have to be careful here. With the fine tip of the quill gripped by a pair of hackle pliers (by far the best way of winding feathers, quills, or anything that might rupture or break), wind the quill up the shank so that the dark edge just touches the light edge and gives you defined banding.

4 Three-quarters (or two-thirds) of the way up the shank, catch in two goose biots by their fine tips on both sides of the shank.

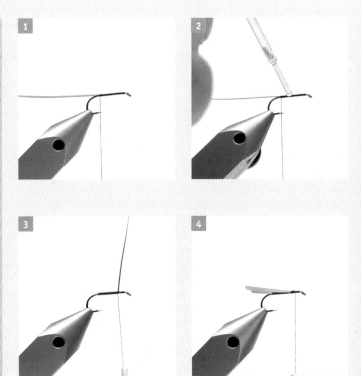

However, the body material presents a problem. First, you need the right peacock quills. When selecting, take an "eye" feather and look just below the blue and green radiating center. Compare the leading edge and the flat side surface and you will be able to determine whether the quill has strong contrasting areas or appears bland. The broad segmented type is the one to go for. Next comes the preparation. I have tried everything from scraping off the fine hair with a razor blade and rubbing it off with an eraser to dissolving it with a peroxide solution (effective, but I then had to anoint the dry, brittle feather with a clear hand cream!). In France you can buy the prepared quills, which are fantastic, from a company called Deveaux. Then all you need to do is to soak them to make them pliable.

Hook: Medium-weight wet fly, 10–14
Thread: Predominantly black, claret red, or olive 8/0–12/0
Body: Stripped peacock quill
Wing buds: Fluorescent orange dyed turkey or goose biots
Thorax cover: Medium pearl Mylar
Thorax: Peacock Ice Dub or peacock herl

MATERIALS

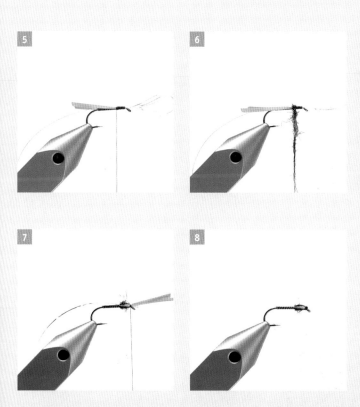

5 Tie in the pearl Mylar thorax cover.

6 Start the dubbing at the point where you caught in the biots—I urge you to craft a noodle style dub so that you achieve a very "tight" thoracic area. Advance the dubbing to just short of the eye. Remember to leave room.

7 Advance the biots and tie down at the point shown. I do this one by one, because it's easier and neater than wrestling with both biots at the same time.

8 Bring the Mylar over the thorax and you are done—apart from taking the pattern from the vise, attaching it to a dryer or clip of some type and adding another layer of instant glue over the quill (as in step 3). Allow to dry for 24 hours.

The author's son, Alex, bends into a feisty small lake rainbow. The ultracalm conditions are perfect for the delicacy afforded by a pattern like the Quill Buzzer.

TACTICS

The slower you fish this design, the more effective it is; I don't necessarily mean a dead halt—although this pattern fished static works brilliantly well—but fished very slowly and simply left to meander around, wind-aided, with you just keeping in touch with the line and leader with hand twist movements.

The addition of another pattern, a heavier one, on the point of a longish leader (say 18–20 in [45–50 cm], for instance) can make all the difference, too, holding up the Quill Buzzer in the target layer so that patrolling trout can intercept.

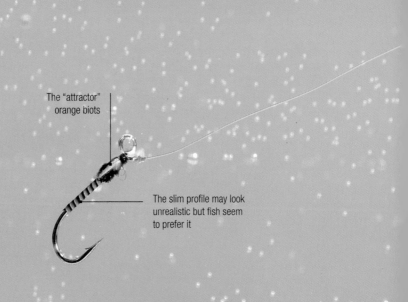

The "attractor" orange biots

The slim profile may look unrealistic but fish seem to prefer it

BEHAVIOR

Chironomidae on U.K. stillwaters are well-documented subjects. The curve of the natural pupa, the segments, the almost prehistoric quality all scream to be imitated—and that is the problem: all too often anglers have tried to convey the insect or the stage with complexity rather than carefully considered simplicity. Today we are constantly in search of the "grail." We use a multiplicity of materials and, as worthy as the effort may be, the more we strive, the less of the life essence of the creature we seem to convey. Patterns like the Quill Buzzer actually do remind trout of the insect. The design embodies life and the vital thing is that the pattern simulates an aspect of the natural, be it in an imminent state of hatching, at the surface, or drifting through the layers.

A midwinter Ellerdine rainbow falls for the charms of a delicate quill midge, fished just under the surface on a hostile, gray day. Ellerdine is a series of small lakes in Shropshire, England, near to the author's home, and the testing ground for a number of patterns.

TACKLE

Unhesitatingly, I will offer my favorite system—a 10 ft (3 m) #5 fly rod with a long-bellied or double-tapered floating fly line. Old-fashioned though these may be, they allow the fisher to pick up more line and re-present at range. This is vital when trying to intercept fast-feeding and moving fish, as they sometimes are when dining on midges. Keep those leaders long—err toward 18 ft (5.4 m) or more.

VARIATIONS

By using different colors of dyed quill—quill takes a dye bath really well—you will be able to grow a really diverse and effective range of designs.

JOHN MORE & OTHERS

Season: *Spring through to late fall, or whenever surface-feeding is observed*

Type of fish: *Brown and rainbow trout*

HOPPER

I have a great affection for this pattern. It was the fly that made sense of fly fishing for me and narrowed the huge divide between stillwater and my beloved rivers. This pattern made me realize I could bring a world of rivers to huge reservoirs and that I didn't have to sacrifice my love of light lines and a single-fly delicate approach in order to catch the occasional trout. In fact, in some instances the light-line approach was actually more desirable than the heavier outfit styles and larger fly use that I saw going on about me.

DIFFICULTY 5/10

MAKING THE FLY

1 Start by selecting the right hackle. Rather than a premium grade, I prefer the softer (and cheaper) Indian cock capes, which will bed the fly down deeper in the surface film.

2 Tie the hackle in first by the stripped stalk. This is the classic way, and it will allow you room to work along the body.

3 Run the thread in a neat smooth layer catching in some pearl Mylar at the hook bend. Form a small "butt" of Mylar—this will emulate the gradually discarded exoskeleton of a hatching fly.

4 In noodle style, dub the seal's fur (sub) body. Try and aim for a semi-loose rope section.

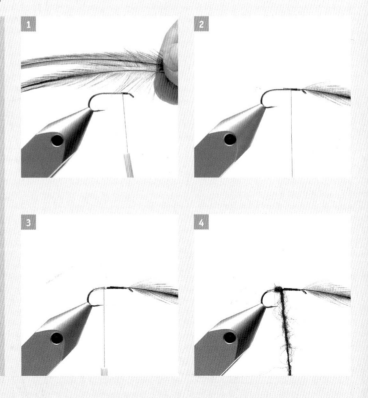

Since those days, this dry fly, together with the Shuttlecock, has formed the backbone of my stillwater dry fly box and the Hopper in all its guises has reigned supreme—and not just on U.K. waters. Friends in the U.S., especially those fishing on western waters, misconstrued my idea of a hopper to their more familiar grasshopper designs, and out of sympathy tried this design nonetheless: they caught a lot of trout on it, especially when fishing rivers. But it is stillwaters where this fly has its forte. It is hard to imagine anything quite so beguiling as drifting amid the great watery expanse of an English reservoir ringed with green meadows, trees, and the gentle lap of water, and fishing a fly like this to the odd trout furrowing the surface—and then breathlessly watching as it vanishes.

Hook: Lightweight—yet wide gape— dry fly (Kamasan B400 for instance) 10–14

Thread: Claret, brown, red, or black 8/0

Hackle: Natural red cock hackle, slightly webby and softer than the usual premium dry fly grades

Butt: Pearl Mylar

Body: Seal's fur (sub) in claret, red, olive, black, orange

Legs: Cock pheasant tail fibers, knotted once, x 6

MATERIALS

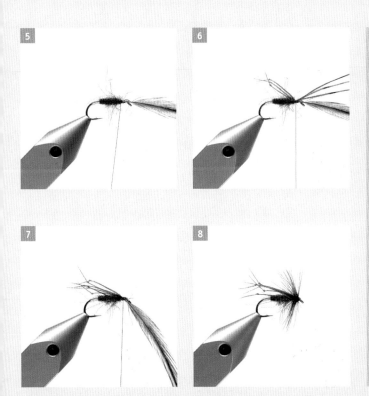

5 The purpose of this is that when it is fashioned around the hook shank in a gradual close spiral it forms a rough segmentation.

6 Now comes the fun part: knot the pheasant tail fibers. A simple overhand knot in the fiber will do it, but try and get that knot as close to the very end as possible. Tie these in bunches of three either side of the shank and so that they project slightly upward.

7 Trim the base and make a smooth area on which to wind the cock hackle.

8 Now wind the hackle. Keep the turns to a minimum—three or possibly four revolutions of hackle, sometimes less. You want to go for a sparse pattern rather than something that is patently overdressed.

TACTICS

I tend to use shorter leaders than in other styles of my stillwater fishing—14 ft (4.2 m) or less. They are quicker to target. I also tend to fish the fly singly or at most two for accuracy.

The other essential is to de-grease the tippet to reduce shine and push it under the surface. U.K. anglers always carry nylon "sinkant"—a mixture of fuller's earth, liquid soap, and glycerol. I find it odd that U.S. fly fishers seem not to. In the U.K. we believe it is the difference between fish and no fish.

If fishing from a float tube or boat, or even the bank, I try to cast as close to the observed rising trout, and aim to the side rather than directly in front. I have found I get far better hookups.

Andy Lush, the well-known South of England angler, about to net a Hopper-deceived trout from one of his favorite lakes, Arlington in Sussex, U.K.

The hackle can fish "in" or "on" the surface depending on your or the trout's preference

The legs are designed to both support and be an attractor

BEHAVIOR

There is, in this instance, no real natural that the fly might look like—or at least I think there isn't. I am told by the great and the good that it is supposed to resemble a small crane fly. I am not sure about you, but I have seen very few red crane flies. Other fishers tell me that it's supposed to represent an adult midge, a *chironomid*. Hmmm. Some midge! And those legs! One thing is certain—it is broadly reminiscent of a whole gamut of surface-oriented insects trapped in the surface, and to have a pattern that covers the entire "chocolate box" can't be all bad, can it? Let the trout make the mistakes. The good thing here is that the legs act as a massive attraction and target for the trout to home in on. As with many natural insects gripped in this way, this element (or six elements) provides a light source that is almost like a dinner-gong for trout.

The trout's eye view of the Hopper.

TACKLE
Strangely, for a stillwater pattern I would fish this particular fly on my river-oriented equipment, using a 10 ft (3 m) #5 fly rod as my main weapon. If you think the fish might be moving quickly and you need accuracy, then a 9 ft 6 in (2.95 m) rod is also excellent. If you have to use a #6 floating line don't worry, but I would not go above this. Use leaders in the 12–15 ft (3.6–4.5 m) category, tapering to 4X–5X. And de-grease the final 8 in (20 cm) by the fly with mud!

VARIATIONS
In essence there are not many, other than colors. But I certainly would, as well as the types mentioned, tie some amber versions with an arc-chrome fluorescent yellow butt—deadly, especially in summer.

GLOSSARY

ANTRON
The trade name of a synthetic trilobal yarn sold under a range of brand names. It can be mixed with other materials and has a wide range of uses in fly tying.

ATTRACTOR
An artificial fly designed to provoke a fish to take through aggression rather than to imitate a natural insect.

BEAD
Placed on the shank of the hook, tungsten and brass beads add weight to a range of wet patterns, especially nymphs.

BIOT
Short, stiff barb from the lead edge of a primary wing feather, usually of a goose or turkey. Used for creating segmented fly bodies, antennae, and tails.

BOBBIN HOLDER
A fly-tying tool used to hold the tying thread and keep it under tension.

BODKIN
A needle set in a handle. Used to apply cement or lacquer to a fly, or to tease out dubbing.

CDC
"Cul de canard" – light, downy feathers from a duck's back used in dry fly tying. They are extremely buoyant, largely because the fine structure of the barbules traps air.

CHALK STREAM
(See spring creek)

CHENILLE
Soft, strung material wrapped around the hook to form a thick body on some flies.

CHIRONOMID
Nonbiting midge. This family of two-winged flies provides an important food source in the larval, pupal, and adult stages, and many fly patterns are based on these.

CREE
Naturally multicolored barred hackle.

CZECH NYMPHING
A style of fishing in which two or three weighted nymphs are fished on a dead drift as close under as short a line as practicable.

DEAD DRIFT
Method of fishing the fly in which the current alone is used to carry it along without any additional movement being imparted to it by the angler. Used in both dry- and wet-fly-fishing techniques.

DECEIVER
An artificial fly tied as a near copy of a particular insect species.

DRIFT FISHING
Method of boat fishing in which the boat is allowed to drift with the wind, or current-aided down a river.

DROGUE
An underwater parachute used to slow down a drifting boat when necessary. When loch fishing, it is held by a cord fixed amidships.

DRY FLY
An artificial fly designed to be fished on or in the surface of the water.

DUBBING
The application of fur (e.g., animal fur, artificial yarn, Antron, etc.) to the tying thread before winding to form an artificial fly body.

DUBBING WAX
A wax used to assist in applying dubbing to the thread.

DUN SUB IMAGO
An imperfect fly of an ephemerid (mayfly family) that has just hatched on the water surface from the nymphal stage. The name refers to its drab color scheme in both wings and body.

EMERGER PATTERN
An artificial dry fly that imitates a hatching insect.

FREESTONE RIVER
A rainfed, spate river, usually with some acidity, having a stony/rocky river bed with few weeds and generally found in mountainous areas.

GAPE
The distance between the point of a hook and the shank.

GRIZZLY
Black-and-white banded (hackle).

HACKLE
A long, pointed cock or hen feather from the bird's neck area, bound around the shank of a fly-hook to represent the legs and thorax of a natural insect. Cock feathers are used in dry flies because their stiff tips assist flotation. Hen feathers are softer and so are used to create the hackle in wet flies to aid movement and attraction.

HACKLE PLIERS
Pliers that grip the hackle securely by the tip in fly tying and facilitate rotation.

HAIR STACKER
Tool for stacking and aligning stiff hairs, such as elk, prior to tying.

HATCH
The simultaneous surfacing of a large number of flies of the same species. To "match the hatch" is to imitate the hatching species as closely as possible at each stage.

HEAD CEMENT
Varnish or glue used to secure the thread and impart a glossy finish.

HERL LONG
Slightly furry, pliant barb of the feather of ostrich, peacock, or similar.

IMITATOR
An artificial fly that is tied to imitate a natural food form.

INSTANT GLUE
Quick-setting glue such as Superglue or Zap-A-Gap.

LARVA
The subaquatic form of some insect species.

LEAD WIRE
Wrapped on the hook shank to create a weighted underbody.

LEADER
A length of nylon that forms the connection between flyline and fly. Can either be tapered, stepped down in sections using various diameters, or a straight nylon length.

MARABOU
Soft, downy feathers used as tail or wing (even body) material to impart movement to a wet fly in the water.

MUDDLER
Fish or insect pattern with a spun, shaped deer hair head.

MYLAR
The trade name of a synthetic, shiny plastic material that is used for fly bodies, tails, and wing cases.

NYMPH
A general term used for an insect between the egg stage and hatching, when the insect lives underwater. Also describes patterns that imitate this stage and fished below the surface.

PALMERED HACKLE
A method of winding the hackle along the hook shank in open turns.

PARACHUTE
A hackle wound horizontally around the vertical base of the wing rather than around the hook shank.

POINT FLY
The bottom fly in a team of flies. Also known as the tail fly.

POST
Upright wing base around which a parachute hackle is wound.

PUPA
The aquatic stage of winged insect species development, occurring between the larval stage and maturity.

RIB
An overbody winding used to create segmentation.

SCUD
Freshwater shrimp.

SHANK
The straight portion of a hook between the bend and the eye.

SPINNER
A mature upwing fly, also known as an imago. The female is described as a spent spinner as she lies inert on the water surface after egg laying.

SPRING CREEK
A stream or river rising from underground springs in limestone hills. The water, which is clear and rich in life forms, usually including trout, runs steadily and at a consistent level because it is only slightly affected by rainfall.

SUB
Abbreviation for substitute. Applies to fly-tying materials where the original is either environmentally unacceptable (e.g., lead) or ethically dubious (e.g., seal fur).

SWISS STRAW
Synthetic substitute for raffia. Used for shell cases on nymph and shrimp patterns.

TINSEL
A thin metallic-colored ribbon that is used to add shine to flies, often as ribbing or for the body.

TIPPET
The thin terminal section of a leader—usually leading to the fly—often knotted to it.

TIPPET SIZE
The X-rating of a tippet indicates its diameter (not breaking strain). The diameter (in thousandths of an inch) plus the X-rating always add up to 11, so a 3X tippet has a diameter of 0.008 in.

VARNISH
Applied to parts of the tied fly to seal and add a glossy finish.

WET FLY
An artificial (often referred to as a "traditional" when wings are added) fly designed to be fished below the surface.

WING CASE
The structure on the back of the immature insect that holds the undeveloped wings.

WIRE
Available in a range of colors and thicknesses. Used to create a weighted underbody or to apply ribbing to flies.

ZONKER STRIP
A thin strip of animal—rabbit, mink, etc.—fur used to create flowing bodies and tails for leech and minnow patterns.

RESOURCES

One of the most frustrating elements in fly tying is having someone quote a distinctive product or item of equipment and then not tell you where to get it. Here, then, are folk and establishments that can provide hard-to-get and innovative products that have stood the test of time, as well as the more mainstream.

ARRICK'S FISHING FLIES

I knew Arrick and his store in West Yellowstone when it was just a small shack off the main drag of the town. Both he and it have grown to provide one of the best selections of materials, particularly chenille's and yarns, anywhere in the world.
37 Canyon St.
P.O. Box 1290
West Yellowstone, MT. 59758
info@arricks.com

BOB MARRIOTT'S FLY FISHING STORE

Situated in Orange County in Southern California, it is hard to imagine a better-stocked store with everything you might wish to find in the mainstream and beyond. A first stop for many of us and, like Arrick's, a great source of knowledge and information.
www.bobmarriottsflyfishingstore.com

COOKSHILL FLY TYING (U.K.)

For all things natural. Steve Cooper is the guru of natural furs and feathers that go to make the classic wet flies and soft hackles. There is none better.
www.cookshill-flytying.co.uk

KAUFMANN STREAMBORN

This well-respected and long-standing cluster of stores in the pacific Western (Washington and Oregon) U.S. is an utterly reliable source of mainstream materials. Great service, great products.
www.kaufmannstreamborn.com

MARC PETITJEAN

This man is my guru for all things CDC. His knowledge and products are just amazing. He is also one of the nicest and most artistic people in our sport.
www.petitjean.com

ROD TYE

Arguably the best classic dyed Irish fur and feather materials in the world today. If you want "subtle," then this is the place to go. (The name alone is reason enough to purchase!)
Invicta House,
Cushlough, Ballinrobe,
Co. Mayo. Ireland
rodtye@eircom.net

ROMAN MOSER

For a host of innovation and mind-blowing materials and ideas I wholeheartedly recommend that you explore the products of one of our finest river anglers in the world today, Roman Moser.
www.romanmoser.com

SIMAN LTD

For the Czech products and nymph-oriented materials, try the products of one of the very finest river fishers in the world today, Jiri Klima. His products can be found with Jan Siman's: there is some truly awesome stuff at this outlet.
Siman Ltd
Kpt. Jarose 1,
326 00 Plzen,
Czech Republic
info@siman.cz

INDEX

ACKNOWLEDGMENTS

A book is not written by just one person; it might say so on the cover, but it is built on a family of support, help, and consummate skill. I am the last one in that process and have relied on the brilliance of others in the team.

My sincere thanks go out to:

Jason Hook: who has always been the gentle and reasoned voice of calm in the odd storm.

Dominique Page: who has put up with an angler's odd ways with sound decisions and a gentle, soothing approach, and has assembled all this so magnificently in the package you see here.

Andrew Perris: the studio photographer—brilliant—and now a firm friend: thanks.

Ian Whitelaw: my editor. We came together late in the day, and he has steered this project and brought succinct sense to my ramblings, musings, and words: "Thank you" is inadequate.

My dear wife Carole, daughter Annabelle, and, of course, Alex, who are the inspiration that drives, and are, simply, my life.

And let's not forget my Black Labrador Midge: the only one that never answers back and agrees with me—mostly.

Also, to all the anglers that I meet and who help in many ways, and make the sport what it is, especially my friends in the U.S. and the Federation of Fly Fishers.

But I would like to especially dedicate this book to the young people of the English Youth Fly-Fishing team—the "world" rivers team. They have been my inspiration and the evangelists of our sport into the future. Fly fishing is in good hands.

And, finally, to fish and wild places, may they both be there for future generations.

Ivy Press would like to thank Charles Jardine for supplying the photographs used to illustrate the text on Tactics and Behavior, with the exception of the following:

Corbis Steve Austin/Papilio: 30, 111; Alan & Sandy Carey/zefa: 171; Joe McDonald: 179.

Alamy Andrew Darrington: 63; Barry Bland: 107; blickwinkel: 123; David R. Frazier Photolibrary, Inc: 151.